ARCHITECTURAL TREASURES OF EARLY AMERICA

★ ★ ★ ★ ★ ★ ★

COLONIAL HOMES IN THE SOUTHERN STATES

ARCHITECTURAL TREASURES OF EARLY AMERICA

COLONIAL HOMES IN THE SOUTHERN STATES

From material originally published as
The White Pine Series of Architectural Monographs
edited by
Russell F. Whitehead and Frank Chouteau Brown

Prepared for this series by the staff of
The Early American Society

Robert G. Miner, Editor
Anne Annibali, Design and Production
Jeff Byers, Design and Production
Nancy Dix, Editorial Assistant
Patricia Faust, Editorial Assistant
Carol Robertson, Editorial Assistant

An
Early
American
Society
Book

Published by Arno Press Inc.

Copyright © 1977 by Arno Press Inc. and The Early American Society, Inc.

Library of Congress Cataloging in Publication Data

Main entry under title:

Colonial homes in the Southern States.

(Architectural treasures of early America : v. 7)
(An Early American Society book)
    1.   Architecture, Domestic—Southern States.
2.   Architecture, Colonial—Southern States.   3.   Architecture—
Southern States.   I.   Miner, Robert G.
II.   Early American Society.   III.   The Monograph series,
records of early American architecture.   IV.   Series.
NA7211.C7   728.3   77-14465

ISBN: 0-405-10070-1 (Arno)   ISBN: 0-517-53272-7 (Crown)
Distributed to the book trade by Crown Publishers, Inc.

CONTENTS

Southern Mansions

SINCE the latter days of the eighteenth century, the first indication of architectural sanity was that rejuvenescence or regeneration of the spirit which must have been behind the earlier expressions of architecture in America. Even though we must accept the English Georgian parentage, this Georgian or Colonial happens to be the only style or method which the colonists understood or desired. That this period architecture was interwoven in our fabric of free government, that it housed the conception and completion of our Constitution, and that it formed a stage background for our Fourth of July orations and the perorations of our politicians, must prove to our ultimate satisfaction that Colonial is our national style of architecture.

The renaissance of Colonial happened at the psychological moment, as all the rebirths in architecture have happened; for while the few architects—and they were few, those of the middle nineteenth century—were content and complacent in their fraternal association with the carpenter, there happened to be a small percentage of this baker's dozen of architects who revolted at this immoral association with that "cocotte" of good taste.

Among these few objectors were the original members of the firm of McKim, Mead & White, for I have found records of sketching trips in the late seventies by Wm. B. Bigelow and by Charles F. McKim; trips made through the old towns of New England, where entire streets of fine examples of the early work had been neglected and undiscovered for more than half a century. There had been a few sporadic attempts to study these examples before this time,

but these attempts were confined mostly to the research work of antiquarians and to a few, a sad corporal's guard, of the small number of practising architects.

These two men of the old firm of McKim, Mead & Bigelow had the prior knowledge of the fine examples of Colonial, and, I believe, with few exceptions, were the first architects to succumb to the charms of the old traditions.

It was about this time, too, that Arthur Little of Boston printed a series of pen and ink sketches for private circulation. This book, unfortunately, has disappeared from the ken of man. I remember, however, the great pleasure which the study of this early set of drawings gave me when I began my wanderings in the pleasant land of Colonial architecture.

I was not more than fifteen years of age when the fondness for these old buildings first inspired me, and during the succeeding seven or eight years I measured and made drawings of the old New England work on holidays and after office hours, during which my time was occupied in tracing and designing those illustrious so-called "Queen Annes" which were actually accepted by architects and laity alike as the supreme expression of good taste in architecture.

The fellows who joined in this quest are to-day scattered throughout the country; indeed, a few of them have mounted *au ciel*. I frequently wonder if Cormer of Seattle, or Charlie Coolidge of Boston, ever remember the rape of the staircase in the old north end of Boston, when we youngsters bribed the complacent tenant to watch for the landlord, and then, with a prepared substitute and a stair-builder,

MOUNT VERNON MANSION, FAIRFAX COUNTY, VIRGINIA
Probably the most notable of Virginia plantations, the home of George Washington

WYE HOUSE, TALBOT COUNTY, MARYLAND. Built about 1780
The original manor-house was built in 1668. A fragment of this is now used as an outbuilding. The main building contains the principal rooms and connects by corridors with one-story wings in which are the library on one side and the domestic offices on the other. The whole facade is two hundred feet in length

"THE GLEBE," POWHATAN COURT, VIRGINIA

An example of the use of a large central dormer with smaller ones
on either side; characteristic of houses of this class in the South

DR. BILDERBECK'S HOUSE, SALEM, NEW JERSEY. Built in 1813

The bead-edged clapboard walls are painted yellow and the trim is white. There has been an unfortunate
20th-century excrescence added at the side. The building is otherwise intact and as sound as when first built

"HOMEWOOD," NEAR BALTIMORE, MARYLAND.   Detail of
Front Portico.   Built in 1809

An example of the second phase of the Southern Georgian.   There is an individuality in the
planning of these Maryland estates to provide for offices, servants' quarters, tool houses, etc.
These were built as story-and-a-half wings, and connected with the main house by one-story
corridors.   This general scheme was as well adapted to town use as it was to the country house

picked out and carried away bodily that beautiful twisted newel-post with the varying carved balusters and mahogany rail. "Pop" Chandler, in whose office we installed the stolen trophy, had numerous fits when we informed him that "a kind lady had given the thing to us." The draughtsmen of the office of that time have since become fat and portly architects, such men as Longfellow and Austin, Ion Lewis and dear old Billy Barry, who in himself was a most delightful Colonial expression. His sketches of ships and of old compositions of eighteenth-century buildings were masterpieces; he knew the intimate detail of a dentilled turn in the cornice, the habits of clapboards and rake-moldings, and the customs and manners of gables and dormers as few other men knew them.

In order to gather sufficient funds for a European trip, it occurred to me that possibly I might acquire such with a few carefully measured drawings of good examples of the Colonial. The plan seemed good and the layouts were not difficult; but I smile to-day when I remember the rocky path ahead of that unsophisticated youngster who expected to achieve Spain and Italy through the easy by-paths of Colonial drawings.

Ware of the *American Architect* would not even look at the proffered sheets; Col. Meyer of the *Engineering Record* wanted to cut them up, though this big-hearted man tried to sell them for me and offered them to Comstock in New York. This effort was more hopeless than the other with Ware in Boston. Then there comes on the screen that fine old soul whose memory many architects still adore—"Pop" Ware, then in Columbia. These drawings suggested something to him, and his students were permitted to look them over as inspirations for their own summer work. After Prof. Ware

"DOUGHOREGAN MANOR," HOWARD COUNTY, MARYLAND
Home of Charles Carroll

had put his seal of approval on these sheets, they were demanded by and sold to the *American Architect*. To-day they form a part of the Georgian Period.

I have wondered in my later days at the difficulties which I had encountered in disposing of these drawings, realizing, of course, that the profession at that time had little, if any, appreciation of the charm and fitness of that phase which has since come to be known as Old Colonial. I have never been able to comprehend the "Old," though I have been told by one of the grandfathers of the profession that I, myself, was responsible for this false appellation. I wish here to disclaim the credit for the misnomer, and will hereafter, being relieved of this anachronism in phraseology, insist that Colonial is the only correct and proper label for those beauties of the eighteenth century which we to-day know with such intimacy.

On my return from the European trip I was amazed and delighted to find a representative of Col. Meyer on the dock, a contract in his hand, and with a demand from the virile West that Wallis be looked up and sent South. With this commission and sufficiently financed, I began my journey south, much as Sir Galahad did in his search for the Holy Grail.

I had been face to face with the great expressions of Europe, and had talked with Vedder, with Abbey, and with others in the ateliers of the E. D. B. A. I knew the museums of Madrid, of Florence, of Paris, and of London; the streets and alleys of all of those Spanish, Italian, and French cities where architecture is at home, and where the street gamins and the proletariat are in complete accord with the architectural expressions of their fathers. With the memories of the old world fresh in my mind, and with added experience and know-ledge, this Southern trip was much the same to me as those side jour-neys which I had made into Brittany, Provence, and through the byways and alleys of the archi-tects' paradise.

The Southern journey led to Fells Point in Baltimore, to Annapolis, Fredericksburg, Va., Wil-liamsburg, and York-town, among others.

I sailed up the York River to Rosewell in a log dugout. How we got there I do not know, but this I remember with pleasure, as I remember the constant courtesy of those Virginia folk, that those at Rosewell permit-ted me to sketch the beautiful details of that supreme expression in architectural history without any objection.

"THE WILLOWS," GLOUCESTER, NEW JERSEY
The walls were built of three-inch planks dovetailed together at the corners. Built about 1720

I encountered some op-position in Fredericksburg when I essayed so politely to ingratiate myself in the good graces of the *grande dame* who pre-sided as chatelaine over Kenmore, but without success, until the sugges-tion of the hotel man tempted me to try the husband while the wife was absent. Those of you who read this, coming out of Boston and remem-bering Dizzy Bridge just about where the Public Library now stands, will chortle with glee when I tell you that because I had been in swimming at Dizzy Bridge I was ad-mitted into the fraternity of old friends by this most charming gentleman. He joined with me in getting results before his wife re-turned.

It is a fact that archi-

"MONTEBELLO," NEAR BALTIMORE, MARYLAND. Built in 1812

The detail, both exterior and interior, was extremely minute in scale and departed far from classic traditions. This house resembles "Homewood," both in scale and character of moldings

tecture does catch some of the characteristics of those people who create it; the manners and customs of the people, who must necessarily express themselves in brick, wood, and stone and color, must be and are reflected in the buildings. Because of this fact, and because of that other fact that the people of this middle South were more often gentlemen than otherwise—gentlemen not only because of their social assurance, but gentlemen because they were sportsmen in every sense of the word,—their architecture shows the reflection; or, rather, their architecture is the physical expression of their own thought and point of view.

There must have been a homey, seignorial atmosphere about the great manor-houses in the heyday of their youth and power that would shame our modern Fifth Avenue magnates, if that were possible. The façades of Westover, Shirley, Brandon, etc., are simple, gentle, and assured, as only the façades of men and women who have assurance of place and family may be gentle and simple. I once saw a thoroughbred girl on the back of a thoroughbred horse, coming up the sward from the James to a thoroughbred house—that of Carter's Grove: a perfect picture and a most natural conclusion, for the house was in the class with both Diana and the horse. And these other types might be, and indeed must be, accepted as the progeny of the more stately and dignified châteaux of the great landowners of Colonial times, for here we find the same completeness, the same constraint against over-adornment.

The streets in the little villages of the South are lined with these charming and restful homes, and you will also find in the type which we will call the outhouses of the great mansions, the same care in design and the same restraint in composition and ornament which are illustrated in the charming Williamsburg, Falmouth, and Fredericksburg examples: all of them supreme in their place, and all of them creating a restful atmosphere such as you may find between the covers of "Cranford."

Have you read "Cranford"? If you have, you may possibly appreciate the charming ladies at Harwood House, Annapolis. If you know this classic, the story of the flower-garden, the dinner to which these charming ladies invited the *wanderlust* youngster, the sweet appreciation of his quest, will appeal to you, even though you have not been invited to church service, as I was invited,—invited to join them in their old high-back pew.

Was George Washington a finer and broader man because of his life at Mount Vernon, or was Mount Vernon and its type, such as we know them, beautiful because of the desires of those old worthies who cussed and smoked and tippled, meanwhile fighting our battles and planning our independence from George of England?

We may find Georgian examples through the shires of England. Cork has some of them; Dublin also, and London is colored with its expression. Georgian, however, and not Colonial, for our Colonial, the son of the Georgian, if you please, has clapboards, porches in Doric and Corinthian or near Corinthian, cornices and modillions, or cornices ornamented with the invention of our own native joiners; for wood to these old men was a servant, and they played in and out through the grain of the woods for their curves and their applied ornaments in such fashion as would have shocked the stolid Britishers of the Georgian times.

The drawings and sketches made of the Southern work suggested a book on the subject, and I was again commissioned to go South, although this first book—and I believe it was the first book published on the Colonial—included sketches made in New England, etc. Those other books of photographs and drawings which followed this publication have added tremendously to our knowledge of Colonial, and in the later days the fellows who, like Deane, Bragdon, Chandler, Brown, Embury, and Bessell, have studied the varying phases and who have written books and articles on the subject, have placed the country under great obligations, for these publications have served their part in the development of good taste in architecture.

GOVERNOUR EDEN HOUSE, EDENTON, NORTH CAROLINA. Built about 1750
The framed overhang construction is most unusual in the Southern colonies

THE PENDELTON HOUSE, NEAR RICHMOND, VIRGINIA
The early Virginia colonists built their houses of wood. A characteristic feature of these early houses was the chimney at each end built outside the house wall for its entire height. The occurrence of the gambrel is not nearly so frequent as in the North, and there are few examples of framing with the overhang

SPRING HOUSE AND DAIRY, ESTATE OF GOODLOE HARPER, BALTIMORE COUNTY, MARYLAND.   Built about 1800

Houses of this type were built near a spring or cold, swift-running brook.   There is a sunken trench all around inside the outside wall about 18 inches deep and 18 inches wide.   The cold water enters at one side of the house and goes out the opposite side.   The water is regulated by a gate so that it will not rise beyond the height of the milk jars, which are set in the trenches

LIBRARY

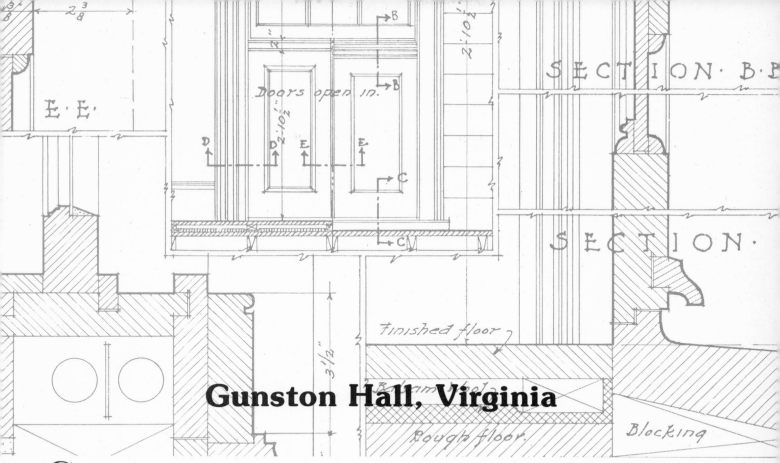

E·E·

Doors open in.

SECTION·B·

SECTION·

Finished floor

Rough floor.

Blocking

Gunston Hall, Virginia

GUNSTON HALL has a familiar and pleasant old world sound and indeed the first "Hall" to bear that name was in Brewood Parish in old Staffordshire, England, in the hamlet called Gunston. George Mason, the Revolutionary patriot, named his Potomac plantation mansion house for that ancestral seat.

There was a George Mason of the Virginia Company in 1620 who may have been the father of the Cavalier, Col. George Mason—the great grandfather of George Mason of Gunston—who embarked for America sometime about 1651 and took up grants of land in Westmoreland, the country extending northward "to the falls of the great river Pawtomake" above what is now Georgetown, District of Columbia. The Cavalier increased his land holdings in 1664 and in 1669 and held the office of County-Lieutenant of Stafford, an office conferred on the class of "gentlemen" or large landholders. The second and the third George Mason added to the large estates of the family which at one time comprised seven thousand acres.

The fourth George Mason, builder of Gunston Hall, was born in 1725. At twenty-five, he married Anne Eilbeck and in 1758 occupied his newly completed mansion—the stately seat of a gentleman of family and culture—in the region with other landed gentry living at Mount Vernon, Belvoir, Stratford and Chantilly. These places were the social centres of that section of the Colonies and their masters maintained a certain state.

George Washington, although seven years younger than George Mason, was a neighbor and a boyhood friend. The private journal of Washington contains many records of his intimacy with Mason. They attended races and balls together, went to hunts and vestry meetings and spent days surveying the bounds of their contiguous lands. Mount Vernon Mansion is on a point only five miles up the river from Gunston Hall but is sixteen miles by road.

When it is considered that the builder of Gunston Hall was called by Jefferson "the wisest man of his generation" and was to Madison the "ablest debator" and to those who have studied his life "a genial, well-read, cultivated gentleman and a man of social parts," it is not difficult to understand that he could not be satisfied with any house which, in respect of design, of material and of finish, was not correct and refined.

The influence of Sir William Chambers, English Architect (1726-1796), is perceptible in many of the homes of the Virginia tobacco and wheat planters. No doubt, George Mason was familiar with the works erected and treatises published by Chambers in England, and perhaps used them as a guide and inspiration in the design of his home. We know that Chambers shares the honors with Chippendale of adapting Chinese forms to decorative furniture and that he adhered to the Anglo-Palladian traditions during the Greek Revival in England. The treatment of the Southeast Room with its "Chippendale" character may well have been inspired from one of Chambers books.

It is not our mission here to surmise, but to set down

GARDEN FAÇADE

notes which may give a hint of the manner of man who built Gunston Hall and point out a few of the facts which are not evident in the photographs and measured drawings.

Gunston Hall is situated on a height on the right bank of the Potomac River about a half mile from the shore and the Southern front commands a full view of the river. From the portico on this front, one descends directly by a long narrow walk, bordered by box, through an extensive garden. The box was said by Lord Balfour of England to be the finest he had ever seen. The house is about three miles from the highway and a private road leads up to the northern front. Here is a portico of four small columns with an arch, forming a Palladian motif. The exposures are actually northwest by west and southeast by east.

We have an extract from an unfinished manuscript of Gen. John Mason, a son of the builder of Gunston Hall, published in Kate Mason Rowland's "*Life of George Mason*" which enumerates the dependencies erected in connection with the mansion. The manuscript reads, "To the west of the main building were, first, the school house, and then a little distance, masked by a row of large English walnut trees, were the stables. To the east was a high paled yard, adjoining the house, into which opened an outer door from the private front, within or connected with which yard were the kitchen, well, poultry houses and other domestic arrangements; and beyond it on the same side were the corn house and granary, servants' houses (negro quarters), hay yard and cattle pens, all of which were masked by rows of large cherry and mulberry trees." We are indebted to this record of the original out-buildings, for the only surviving evidence is the stone well-curb.

Gunston Hall was erected in the adapted Georgian style. It suffered some defacements after it passed out of the hands of the Mason family. The house was restored some time ago.

The plan of the house is the most common of Colonial types—four rooms to a floor with a transverse stair hall. The hall is spacious and is of a width in proportion to the total depth and is perfectly symmetrical although the stair rises along one wall and lands on the other so that the interior spaces are unbalanced. The Southeast Room, the Drawing-room, is the most elaborate.

The rooms on the second floor open on each side of a hall which runs at right angles to the hall below and terminates at each gable end of the house. These rooms are small and low-pitched with dormer windows and wide low window seats. A steep ladder leads up from the hall into the attic. This upper region is lighted and ventilated by a round window in each gable end of the house. The walls are made of large red brick laid up in Flemish bond. The angles of the walls are emphasized by raised blocks or quoins of cut stone. This treatment is a characteristic of the late Renaissance in England. The walls are terminated with well designed cornices of wood, which on the end elevations become large coves, and are painted white in conjunction with the window frames to give pleasant contrast to the façades.

PORCH—SOUTHERN FAÇADE

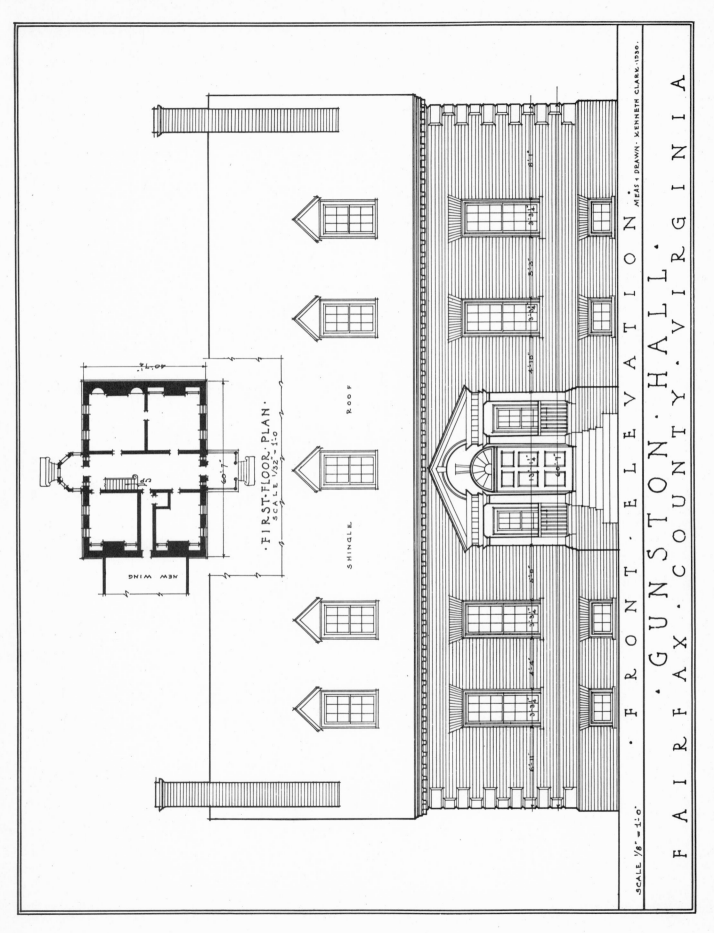

·FIRST·FLOOR·PLAN·
SCALE 1/32" = 1'-0

ROOF

SHINGLE

NEW WING

40'-1½"

60'-7"

·FRONT·ELEVATION· MEAS + DRAWN · KENNETH CLARK · 1930 ·

SCALE ⅛" = 1'-0'

·GUNSTON·HALL·VIRGINIA·
FAIRFAX·COUNTY·

CORNICE DETAIL

THE NORTHERN FAÇADE

The window openings are notably tall in proportion, about 2½ to 1. Mullions and transoms had gone out of general use about this time in England and sash windows were introduced. In Gunston Hall, the sash windows are placed almost flush with the outer face of the walls.

The roof pitch is higher than is usual in examples of the Georgian style, but this fact has been grossly exaggerated in the sketches and drawings which have appeared heretofor. Dormer windows take the place of the windows in the gables of the Jacobean period and so we find the second floor rooms lighted by ten dormer windows placed over the windows and openings of the first story.

As usual, tradition and gossip have attributed the fine wood carving and mouldings of the interior of Gunston Hall to "convict craftsmen from England," to actual "importation of the finished products from England," etc. We do not know the name of the woodworker, but we feel sure that he was not left to his own devices in the execution of the design, for the details are too well studied in relation to the proportion of each room and each opening in each room, to have been left to the workman or ordered from "stock" from across the sea. The door enframement with pilasters was unusual before the Revolution—there are examples in Charleston, South Carolina, and Maryland, but they all date after 1758. Gunston Hall has, also, a most elaborate window treatment, internally; a pair of pilasters with full entablature. The employment of open semi-circular niches, a variant of the semi-circular door head, is first found in

GARDEN FAÇADE

American domestic architecture in this house. It was the woodworkers and the carpenters who gave the decorative accessories of Colonial houses their chief distinction.

Of all the seats on the Potomac River, Gunston Hall is the most well studied adaptation of the English Georgian style and presents a splendid picture of a Tidewater Virginia house. Although only a story and a half high, and simple in design, it was evidently the work of one who knew and valued the virtues of proportion and dignity and delicacy of detail. Here as usual architectural merit can not vie with historical interest and Gunston Hall will always be known and venerated for being the scene of some of those early expressions of Colonial disaffection which finally led to the War of the Revolution. George Mason will always be remembered as the author of the Bill of Rights and the Constitution of Virginia, and for his intimate association with the Declaration of Independence. We feel that, to his other cultural accomplishments, including the design of the State Seal of Virginia, credit should be bestowed upon Mason of Gunston for his share in the production of his important house. He died at home in 1792 and is buried on the property, as was the custom in his day.

Gunston Hall is one of the eighteenth century country mansions of the South still standing as a symbol of a life which was on a grand scale for the few—made possible by the slavery of the many. "There are said to have been five hundred persons on the estate, including the several quarters."—"*Life of George Mason.*" An excess of cheap labor over a long period usually results in the blossoming of a high culture and here that result is exemplified.

HOUSE VIEWED FROM THE GARDEN

DETAIL OF NORTHERN PORCH

PORCH DETAIL—NORTHERN FAÇADE

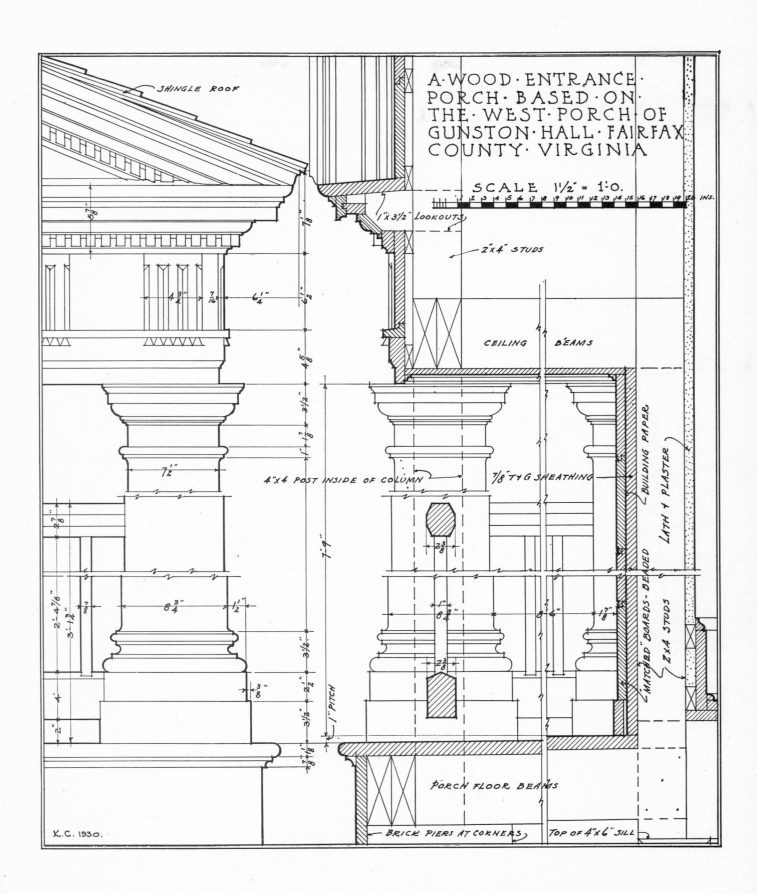

SHINGLE ROOF

A·WOOD·ENTRANCE·
PORCH·BASED·ON·
THE·WEST·PORCH·OF·
GUNSTON·HALL·FAIRFAX·
COUNTY·VIRGINIA

SCALE 1½" = 1'·0.

1 2 3 4 5 6 7 8 9 10 11 12 13 14 15 16 17 18 19 20 INS.

1"x 3½" LOOKOUTS

2"x 4" STUDS

CEILING BEAMS

BUILDING PAPER

LATH & PLASTER

4"x 4 POST INSIDE OF COLUMN

7/8" T & G SHEATHING

2" MATCHED BOARDS · BEADED

2"x 4 STUDS

PORCH FLOOR BEAMS

K.C. 1930.

BRICK PIERS AT CORNERS

TOP OF 4"x 6" SILL

HALL

STAIRCASE DETAIL

26

STUCCO   WOOD

STONE

· D E T A I L · O F · F R O N T · P O R C H ·

SCALE 3/8" = 1'-0"

MEAS ↑ DRAWN ~ KENNETH CLARK '30

· G U N S T O N · H A L L ·

· F A I R F A X · C O U N T Y · V I R G I N I A ·

THE DRAWING ROOM
GUNSTON HALL, FAIRFAX COUNTY
VIRGINIA

MEASURED DRAWINGS *from*
The George F. Lindsay Collection

CABINET AND CORNICE

DOORWAY—DRAWING ROOM

WINDOW
DETAIL

WAINSCOT DETAIL

WINDOW DETAIL

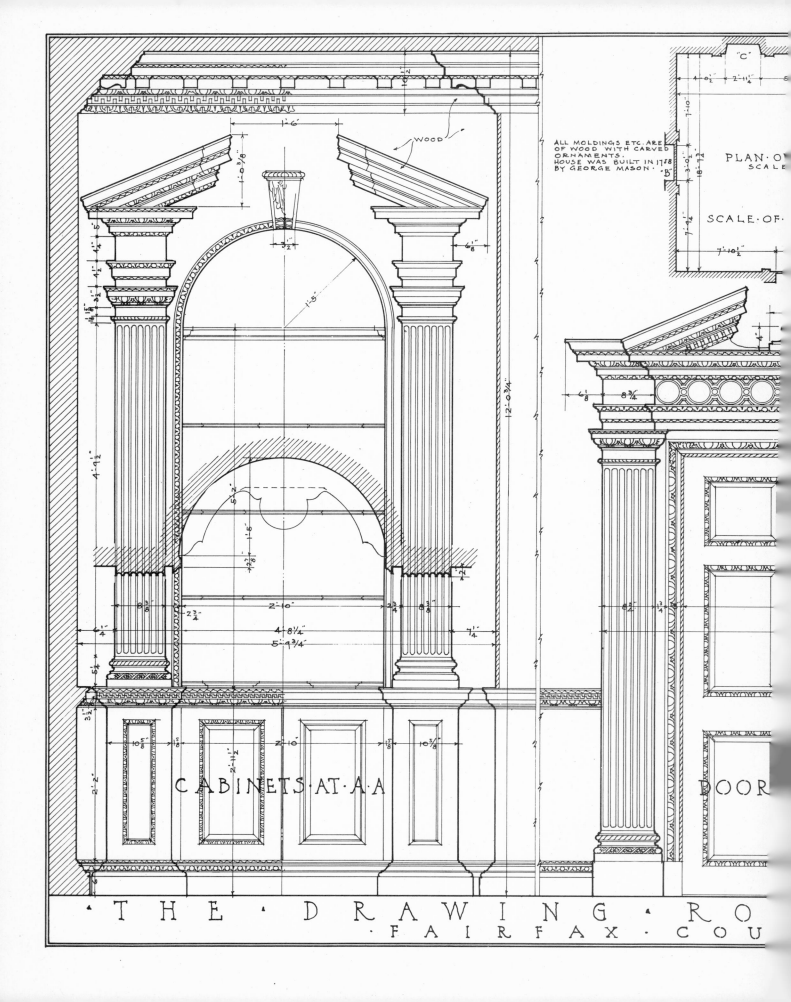

ALL MOLDINGS ETC. ARE
OF WOOD WITH CARVED
ORNAMENTS.
HOUSE WAS BUILT IN 1758
BY GEORGE MASON.

WOOD

PLAN O

SCALE

SCALE · OF

C·A·B·I·N·E·T·S· AT · A·A

D O O R

· T H E · D R A W I N G · R O

· F A I R F A X · C O U

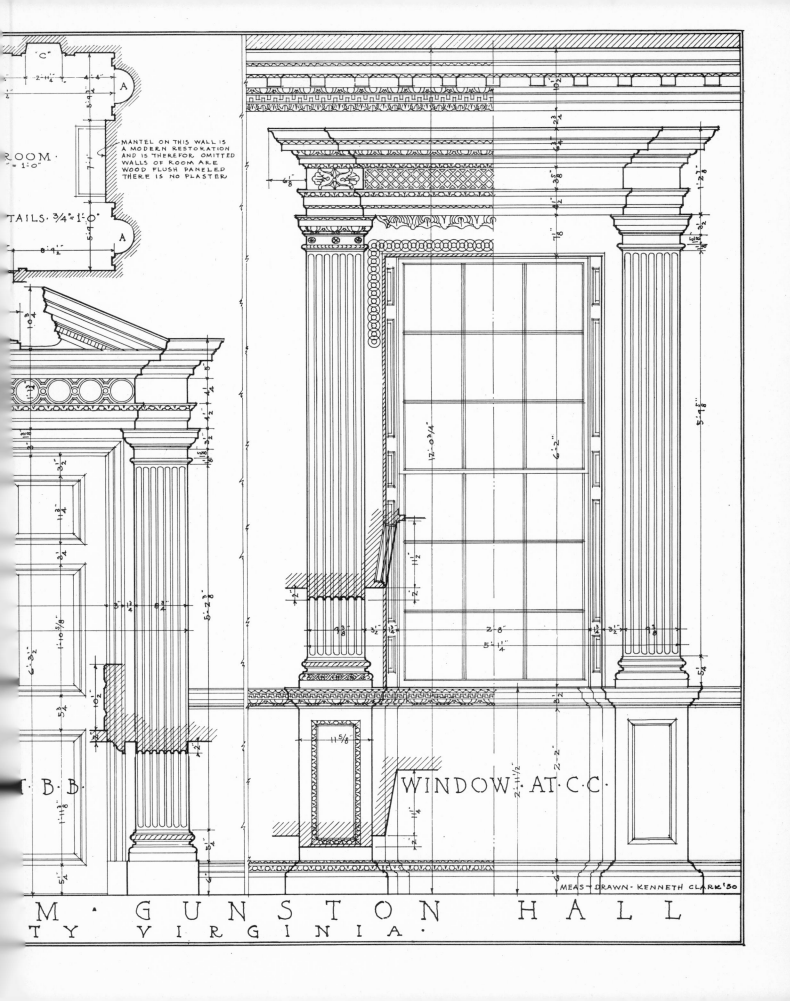

MANTEL ON THIS WALL IS
A MODERN RESTORATION
AND IS THEREFOR OMITTED
WALLS OF ROOM ARE
WOOD FLUSH PANELED
THERE IS NO PLASTER

WINDOW · AT · C · C ·

MEAS · DRAWN · KENNETH CLARK '30

M · GUNSTON HALL

TY VIRGINIA ·

11 5/8

HOUSE AT 711 PRINCESS STREET,
ALEXANDRIA, VIRGINIA

DOORWAY DETAIL

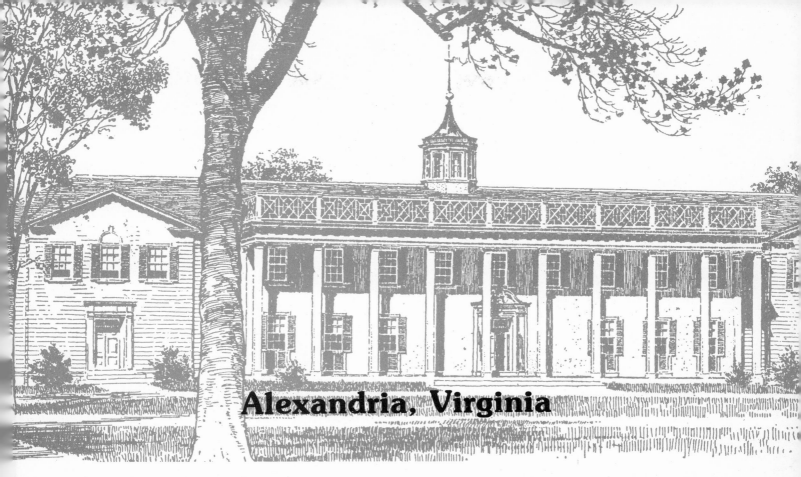

Alexandria, Virginia

ALEXANDRIA, like several other early settlements in America, might have been, but for a whim of Fate, one of the great ports of the Atlantic seaboard. The tide of immigration to the new continent touched the cove that nestled here under the Potomac's high banks, eddied about it for a time, and then swept on to make a Baltimore.

In July, 1608, Captain John Smith and fourteen companions imbued with some of his own intrepid spirit of exploration, sailed up the Potomac River and were the first white men to look upon the site of what was to become Alexandria. They saw merely a small encampment of Doeg Indians, a tribe of the Algonquins, who were friendly and hospitable.

By 1631 there had gathered in the neighborhood a few settlers, who built a tobacco storehouse and called the hamlet Belle Haven. In 1669 Robert Howison obtained a patent for land upon which the little cove settlement was situated, but instead of taking it up, sold the patent to John Alexander, a Stafford planter, for the consideration of 6000 lbs. of tobacco. Not until 1695 was there a settlement upon the grant under the patent, when Thomas Pearson sailed up the river and located upon Pearson's Island, and it was over half a century later, in 1749, that William Ramsay, John Carlyle and associates founded Alexandria.

On March 9, 1780, a government was set up, Alexandria being then over thirty years old. The town spread itself upon a high plateau, extending from Oronoco Creek and its marsh on the north and northwest, to the river shore on the east, and to what was known as the White Oak Swamp on the southwest and south.

It was a town marked by deep loyalty to the Crown, if we may judge by the names given its streets. Royal and Fairfax were the two long streets, crossed by Cameron, King, Queen, Prince, Princess, Duke and Duchess. These shorter cross streets, cutting through to reach the cove below, rounded off the sharp edge of the bluff which had long formed the line of demarcation between the cove and the high plateau. Later on, when loyalty to the King gave place to national self-consciousness, the streets reflected no less definitely the heroes of the new republic, in Wolfe, Wilkes, Pitt, St. Asaph and Patrick Henry, for whom a double measure of pride was expressed in the naming of two streets.

Tobacco was the chief product of the surrounding countryside, and there is probably not an acre within the town limits that has not produced its hundredweight of good Oronoco. With a good harbor and the ability to produce something that the outside world wanted, Alexandria grew rapidly as a trading port for foreign commerce.

Then came the event that proved to be the turning point in the town's march of progress. In August, 1814, two British frigates sailed up the river and took the town. Fort Warburton, designed to protect the community from such an attack, had just been depleted by a withdrawal of troops, and the officer in charge, feeling that resistance would be futile, blew up his

THE "LIGHT HORSE" HARRY LEE HOUSE AND 609 CAMERON STREET, ALEXANDRIA, VIRGINIA

arsenal and abandoned the fort. The invaders looted the town, carrying off quantities of tobacco and grains stored in the port warehouses, and Alexandria's commercial activities suffered a blow from which they never fully recovered. Meanwhile, her rival port, Baltimore, forged ahead, and Alexandria's promised greatness became merely something that might have been. To complete the wreck of great hopes, a fire swept the town in 1827, burning fifty-three houses.

Alexandria's loss, however, is perhaps the gain of architectural students and antiquarians today, for in the little town the march of progress has not swept aside so much of the simple, lovingly detailed work of the late eighteenth century and the early years of the nine-

teenth as in other places where the work of these years has so largely been destroyed in the making of what were fondly thought to be improvements.

Most widely known among the buildings that still remain, wholly or in part, are three that have unusual significance, not only architecturally but as settings for historical events in the early days of the republic. These are Christ Church, the Carlyle House and Gadsby's Tavern. No student thinks of Alexandria apart from these three great landmarks; but, there are other bits that should not be lost to architectural history—a cornice here, an entrance doorway there, a naive bit of wood construction. It is with this thought in mind that the present selection of material is brought together, stressing less the better known work, which has appeared from time to time elsewhere, than some minor details that might otherwise be overlooked and soon pass into oblivion.

Nevertheless, the background of all this work, the flavor of Alexandria, can best be conveyed as relating to her three great landmarks. They, of course, rather than any minor building or unrelated detail, bring to a focus those faraway days on the Potomac—their intensity, the resolute single-mindedness of the men who made them epochal, the innate dignity and taste of their unsophistication, the craftsmanship that so evidently found real joy in itself.

Christ Church, Alexandria, scarcely less than Pohick Church itself, bears an aura of close association with George Washington. He was a vestryman of both churches—his father, Augustine Washington, had been a vestryman of Truro Parish before him—and when Christ Church was opened for worship, purchased his pew for the sum of £26:10:8. Tradition has it that both he and Thomas Jefferson had a hand in the design of Christ Church, though it seems more likely that the building was chiefly the work of James Wren, said to have been a descendent of Sir Christopher.

The church was started about 1765, the contract for its erection being awarded to James Parsons for £600. But, like many of the early churches, it was long in the building, being finished only in 1773 after Parsons had given up the task and Col. John Carlyle had undertaken, in 1772, to complete it for the additional sum of £220. On February 27, 1773, it was finally completed in its original form and dedicated. The gallery was added about 1800 and the tower somewhat later. In design, Christ Church bears a strong resemblance to the later and perhaps better known Pohick Church, differing chiefly in the tower that was added later and a pedimented Palladian window at the opposite end. This similarity of design is not surprising, considering the fact that George Washington himself made the drawings for Pohick Church, and, being a vestryman of Christ Church at the time, had access to Wren's drawings for the earlier building.

It was on the green in front of Christ Church that George Washington, talking earnestly with a few of his friends and neighbors of the tea thrown overboard in Boston Harbor, definitely committed himself to the policy of resistance—and the birth of a new nation became imminent.

A hundred years later, upon the same church green, on a Sabbath morning in May, a retired soldier stood

CHRIST CHURCH, ALEXANDRIA, VIRGINIA

HOUSE ON CORNER OF FAIRFAX AND
WOLFE STREETS, ALEXANDRIA, VIRGINIA

THE FAIRFAX HOUSE
CAMERON STREET,
ALEXANDRIA, VIRGINIA

ENTRANCE DETAIL
THE FAIRFAX HOUSE,
ALEXANDRIA, VIRGINIA

talking with his friends and neighbors. Besought by all, Robert E. Lee here tacitly accepted the command of the Armies of the Commonwealth.

The Carlyle House, second of Alexandria's hallowed landmarks, lately a part of the Braddock Hotel on Fairfax Street, was built by John Carlyle in 1745, upon the foundations of what had been an old stone fort, erected possibly as early as 1638. Carlyle was a prosperous merchant, as may be surmised from the fact that he built this mansion when but twenty-five years old.

Colonel John Carlyle, a close friend of George Washington's, who had married one of the Fairfax family, made his home a center of the social and political life of the day. Here we find gathered such figures in the nation's history as Thomas Jefferson, Aaron Burr, John Marshall, Charles Carroll, John Paul Jones, and James Rumsey, inventor of the first steamboat.

Gadsby's Tavern, third of the architectural monuments by which Alexandria is known, was one of the great stopping places between north and south in the days when stage coaches rumbled over the King's Highway. Originally called Claggett's Tavern, it was built by John Wise in 1792, and few travelers from Williamsburg, Richmond and the south passed by it on their way to Philadelphia without partaking of its widely famous hospitality. Here in the great ballroom, which is now forever preserved against disintegration in the American Wing of the Metropolitan Museum of Art, were held the famous Birthnight Balls, in honor of the

King and Queen. And here, growing out of that early custom, was instituted in 1798 the first public celebration of Washington's Birthday, with the beloved General himself present.

Lafayette was an honored guest at Gadsby's in 1824 —his second visit to Alexandria, for in 1777 he passed through the town on his way to join Washington's army.

Today Alexandria, like Williamsburg, turns her thoughts back to the great days of old. What can a mere future offer to the town which was George Washington's post-office, his place of voting? Here he had his surveyor's office, here brought for sale the produce of his farms. It was here he came to attend Masonic Lodge. Into Alexandria's streets often rolled the coach from Mount Vernon, bringing the family to some social gathering at Colonel Carlyle's or to a dance at Gadsby's Tavern. Here dwelt Dr. Laurie, who attended all Washington's people by contract at £15 the year; Dr. Craik and Dr. Elisha Dick, both of whom attended the General in his last illness. It was from Alexandria that Washington as the young surveyor had set out upon his Western expeditions, and, later, to fight in the wars with the French. He represented the town in the House of Burgesses, surveyed its streets, was a member of its Town Council, and here, on the steps of Gadsby's, the General held his last military review.

Alexandria looks backward, proud of her glorious past, and we, standing afar off, would share her pride, for what was hers is now the heritage of all of us.

ENTRANCE DETAIL
OLD CITY TAVERN,
ALEXANDRIA, VIRGINIA

HOUSE AT NUMBER 711 PRINCE STREET,
ALEXANDRIA, VIRGINIA

THE LEE AND BURSON HOUSES—ORONOCO STREET—ALEXANDRIA, VIRGINIA

ENTRANCE DETAIL
HOUSE AT NO. 711 PRINCE STREET,
ALEXANDRIA, VIRGINIA

The COLROSS HOUSE
ALEXANDRIA, VIRGINIA

CENTRAL PORTION OF FRONT ELEVATION

REAR DOORWAY

MEASURED DRAWINGS *from*
The George F. Lindsay Collection

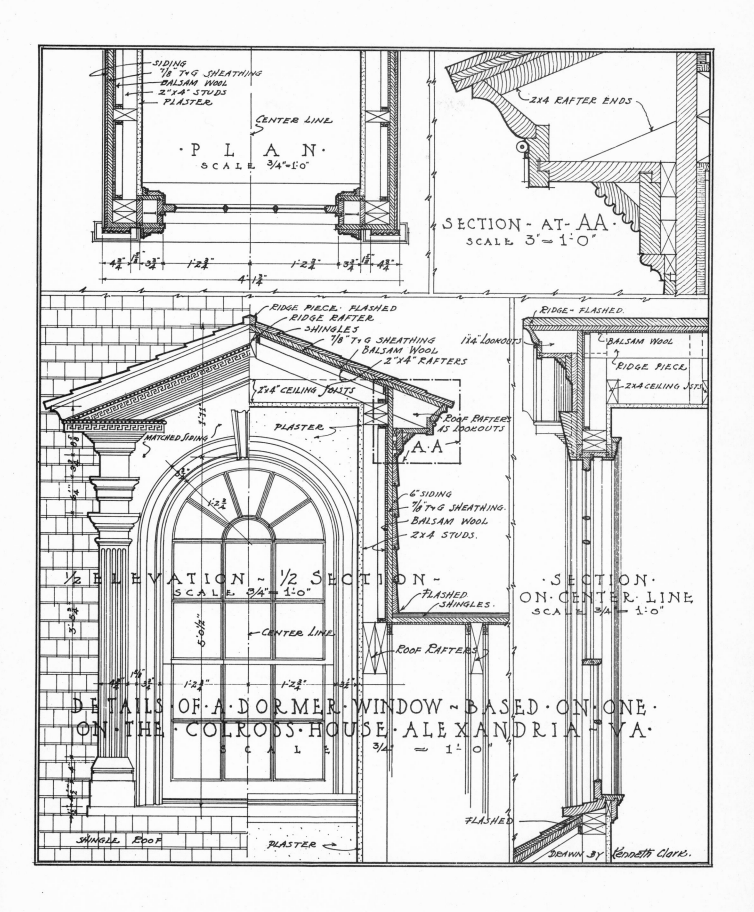

SIDING
7/8" T+G SHEATHING
BALSAM WOOL
2"x4" STUDS
PLASTER

CENTER LINE

· P L A N ·
SCALE 3/4"=1'0"

2x4 RAFTER ENDS

· SECTION · AT · AA ·
SCALE 3"= 1'0"

RIDGE PIECE · FLASHED
RIDGE RAFTER
SHINGLES
7/8" T+G SHEATHING
BALSAM WOOL
2"x4" RAFTERS

1"x4" LOOKOUTS

RIDGE · FLASHED.

BALSAM WOOL

RIDGE PIECE

2x4 CEILING JSTS.

2"x4" CEILING JOISTS

PLASTER

ROOF RAFTERS
AS LOOKOUTS

A A

MATCHED SIDING

6" SIDING
7/8" T+G SHEATHING.
BALSAM WOOL
2"x4" STUDS.

½ · ELEVATION ~ ½ · SECTION ·
SCALE 3/4"= 1'0"

· SECTION ·
ON · CENTER · LINE
SCALE 3/4"= 1'0"

CENTER LINE

FLASHED
SHINGLES.

ROOF RAFTERS

DETAILS · OF · A · DORMER · WINDOW ~ BASED · ON · ONE ·
ON · THE · COLROSS · HOUSE · ALEXANDRIA ~ VA ·
S C A L E   3/4" = 1'·0"

SHINGLE   ROOF

PLASTER →

FLASHED

DRAWN BY Kenneth Clark.

45

MAIN CORNICE

46

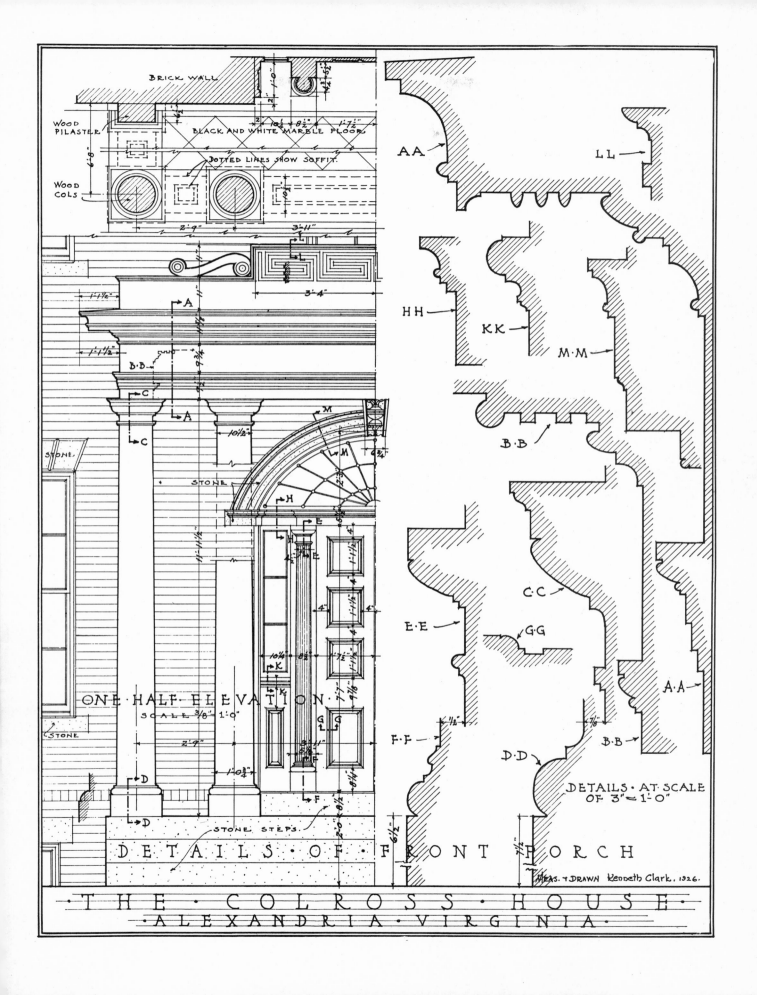

BRICK WALL

WOOD PILASTER

BLACK AND WHITE MARBLE FLOOR

DOTTED LINES SHOW SOFFIT.

WOOD COLS

STONE.

AA

LL

HH

KK

MM

B·B

C·C

G·G

E·E

F·F

D·D

A·A

B·B

ONE·HALF·ELEVATION·
SCALE 3/8"= 1'-0"

STONE

STONE

STONE STEPS

DETAILS·AT·SCALE
OF 3"= 1'-0"

MEAS. + DRAWN Kenneth Clark. 1926.

DETAILS · OF · FRONT · PORCH

·THE · COLROSS · HOUSE·
·ALEXANDRIA · VIRGINIA·

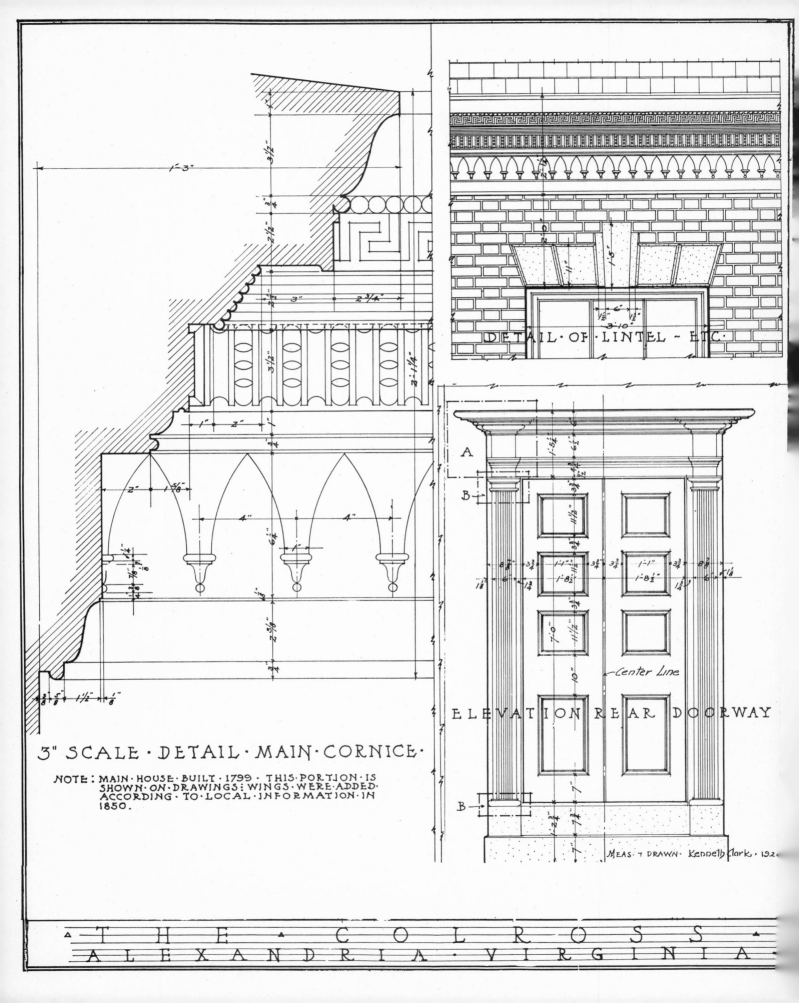

DETAIL·OF·LINTEL~ETC.

A

B

Center Line

ELEVATION·REAR·DOORWAY

B

3" SCALE·DETAIL·MAIN·CORNICE·

NOTE: MAIN·HOUSE·BUILT·1799·THIS·PORTION·IS
SHOWN·ON·DRAWINGS; WINGS·WERE·ADDED·
ACCORDING·TO·LOCAL·INFORMATION·IN
1850.

MEAS. + DRAWN· Kenneth Clark · 192

▲·T H E·▲·C O L R O S S·▲
A L E X A N D R I A·▲·V I R G I N I A·

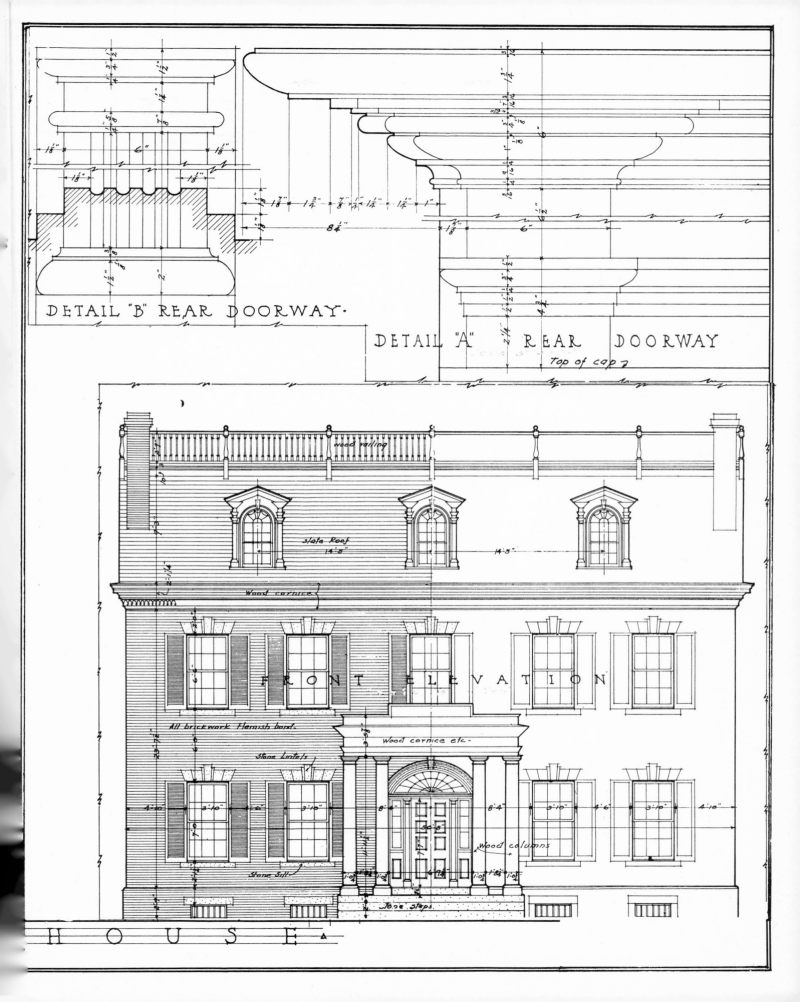

DETAIL "B" REAR DOORWAY.

DETAIL "A" REAR DOORWAY

Top of cap

FRONT ELEVATION

Wood railing

Slate Roof

Wood cornice

Wood cornice etc.

All brickwork Flemish bond.

Stone Lintels

Wood columns

Stone Sill

Stone Steps

H O U S E

HOUSE AT NUMBER 18 ORANGE STREET, NEW CASTLE, DELAWARE

"THE OLD DUTCH HOUSE" (ABOUT 1665), NEW CASTLE, DELAWARE

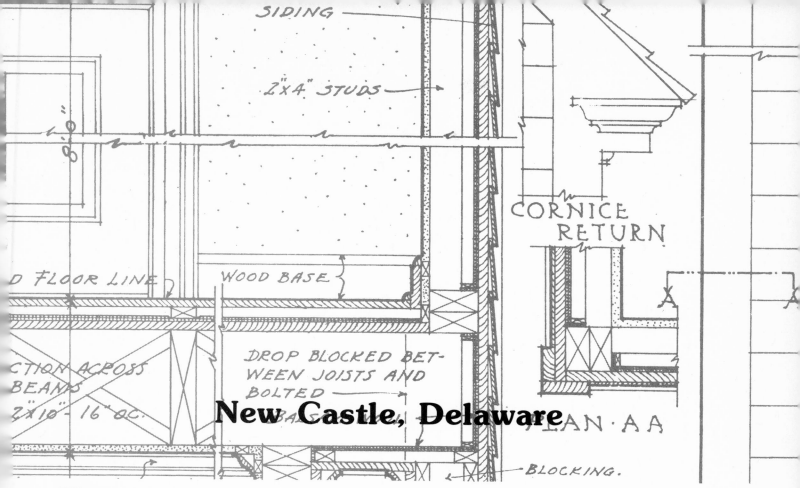

SIDING

2"x4" STUDS

CORNICE
RETURN

D FLOOR LINE

WOOD BASE

DROP BLOCKED BET-
WEEN JOISTS AND
BOLTED

CTION ACROSS
BEAMS
2"x10"- 16" OC.

BLOCKING.

New Castle, Delaware

THERE are few communities to-day which have retained their early American flavor as completely as has New Castle, Delaware. The examples of our colonial architecture in such centers as Boston and Philadelphia and even in Baltimore are so surrounded by present-day business, or lie isolated without any surroundings, that they can give little of the feeling of the actual community which existed when they were built. Quebec, Salem, Charleston and New Orleans do present, each in certain quarters, this sense of the completeness of the community, but New Castle, being a small town, presents the architecture of the middle colonies even more completely than do these other cities of their respective sections.

Though small now and comparatively little known, New Castle was up to the early part of the nineteenth century quite an important place and her commerce brought considerable wealth to her citizens. Her history had gone back to the earliest settlements, to the time of New Sweden and New Netherland. In fact, at the time Henry Hudson discovered what he termed the "North River"—our Hudson River—he also sailed up the "South River"—to-day the Delaware—and it was on that discovery that the Dutch, for whom Hudson was navigating, based their claims of ownership. However, they were slow to act and the Swedes were the first to establish a colony on the banks of the South River, calling the district New Sweden.

The Dutch did not look upon this settlement with much favor and after the Swedes had been established some eleven years Governor Peter Stuyvesant of New Netherland, in 1651, acting partly on instructions from Holland and largely in accordance with his own vigorous instincts, decided to take active measures to protect the Dutch claims. Accordingly he proceeded personally to New Sweden and established Fort Casimir, very near the site of the present town. There followed various turns of fortune for the fort. The Swedes captured it in 1654, but the Dutch came back and in 1655 gained all of New Sweden, or Delaware, and renamed the settlement Fort Amstel, making it the seat of the Dutch government for the local colonies.

Disease and famine as well as a constant fear of the English caused most of the inhabitants to leave and in 1664 the English seized the whole district without much effort, again changing the name of the principal settlement, this time to New Castle. As New Castle it was frequently the meeting place of the legislature and later became the capital of the colony when Delaware was separated from Pennsylvania.

During the colonial days and the years of the Revolution the town played its part in making history. Two of the signers of the Declaration of Independence were residents, while a third had been born in New Castle.

And yet with this imposing background, as rich as that of many towns which are quite large to-day, New Castle at the end of the eighteenth century was as important as it probably ever will be. The principal in-

AMSTEL HOUSE—BUILT ABOUT 1730—NEW CASTLE, DELAWARE

dustrial growth of the district is being assimilated by Wilmington, six miles to the north. While there are some factories with their resultant nondescript housing, they are all grouped near the branch-line railroad which comes in to the west of the town proper. The compact older portion is still complete and removed from too much "progress."

Around the Common, which remains as an open park in the center of the town, are the public buildings. There is the old Court House, one wing of which is supposed to have been built about 1680, though the main portion dates from 1707. It was this building which served as a center for a twelve-mile radius which established the "northern boundary of the colonies on the Delaware," the arc which still is on the maps. Not far behind the Court House is the Episcopal Church, parts of which were built in 1701 and 1705.

To the east of the Court House is the very interesting square building generally known as the Town Hall, but which has been put to various uses from time to time. Once it was the terminus of some sort of railroad and again it formed the end of a shed which covered the town market; at that time the fire engine was kept there and the upper floor was used as a town hall or common room. This three-story building, a perfectly simple square brick structure with its charmingly proportioned cupola and the balustraded deck, is as dignified and satisfying a public building as one can find remaining from the colonial period.

One of the principal residential streets is Orange Street, running along the western side of the Common. At Number 2 facing one end of the Court House, is the house now occupied by Dr. Booker but known historically as the Kensey Johns house, having been built for that gentleman in 1790. The facade is extremely simple but with a fenestration which gives great dignity. The low addition to the right adds considerable interest to the house; it was built as an office for Attorney Johns. This wing contains an entrance hall and one room, a room which with its delightful

WINDOW DETAIL—AMSTEL HOUSE (1730)

AMSTEL HOUSE—MAIN FACADE

Built about 1730

PANELLING IN AMSTEL HOUSE

CORNER IN MAIN ROOM
AMSTEL HOUSE

proportions and arched ceiling testifies to the taste of the builder. The main part of the house has the hall and stairs to the right, with a connecting door to the office, and on the left the living and dining rooms. The kitchen and service rooms are in a wing at the rear.

The panelling and mantels in the two principal rooms are simple, with rather Georgian character in the moldings. The other walls of these rooms are plastered with a dado band carried around, vigorous moldings on the door trims and panelled reveals at the windows. The stairs are interesting, particularly for the very simple manner in which the handrail forms a cap for the newel post.

On the facade we notice one peculiarity which is found in several other houses at New Castle; the marble lintels over the windows, though cut in profile to resemble a flat arch with a keystone, are really of one piece and without any cutting to imitate joints.

The owner is justly proud of the key plates and handles on the main doors, for it is maintained that they are the only ones of that particular design except those at Mount Vernon. In fact, a few years ago, he gave one of these to replace one that had disappeared from Mount Vernon.

Along this same street are several interesting brick facades. These are all similar in design, each has a simple, well-fenestrated wall, a sturdy, well-designed doorway, some richness at the cornice and usually a dormer with pilasters and a small pediment. With their interior panelling, even in rather simple, small rooms, they show the refinement which went with the general affluence of the town during its heyday.

Also on Orange Street is a remainder of the earlier settlement, of a time nearer the pioneer days. It is a little house with its eaves not many feet above the sidewalk and is known as "The Old Dutch House" was built near the middle of the seventeenth century.

On the other side of the Common and one block beyond is the Strand, another street which was favored as the location for many of the better houses. This street runs more or less along the water front with the back yards of one side continuing down to the river in many places. It is on the Strand that we find the most pretentious house in New Castle, the Read house,

Near the Read house is the four-story building known as the "Parish House." It was built for Charles Thomas a very few years after the completion of the Read house. The facade facing the Strand is similar in detail to many others in the town, the pedimented doorway, the one-pieced keystoned lintels, the modil-

CUPOLA OF THE TOWN HALL AND MARKET

THE VAN DYCK HOUSE—NUMBER 400 DELAWARE STREET—NEW CASTLE, DELAWARE

lioned cornice and the single dormer. It does differ in that the doorway is in the middle instead of at one side where it would have permitted the maximum width for a principal room entered from the hallway. However, as it stands on a corner we find that the side elevation becomes quite important, though the designer seemed content with the balance of the front and made little attempt at an axial treatment on the side. The gable, spanning the broader dimension, is cut off at the top by a narrow deck or walk which was probably used for watching the shipping.

The detail of the doorway shows the moldings and ornament which are almost identical with those of the Read house and were undoubtedly done by the same

workmen. Few surfaces were left plain. Facias were treated with regular series of gouges, half-round moldings were carved with rope-like grooves and pitted with auger holes, while dentil courses were replaced by intricately devised bands of great richness.

In many ways the most interesting house in New Castle is Amstel House. Very strongly Dutch in the feeling of its detail, it was built about 1730. The wide gable with an angle of about 29 degrees spans what is the main front, though now on a minor street. The rather heavy doorway, the wide muntins and the large curved frieze surface are more like various houses in and around Philadelphia than those in New Castle. There is a great deal of panelling on the interior and it too has a heaviness which is not found in the other houses, though at the same time it is quite interesting.

The house at Number 400 Delaware Street just opposite Amstel House, was built for Nicholas Van Dyck in 1799. It has in recent times been divided for two families by changing a window into a doorway as is seen in the illustration. The mantel is quite ornate and in the piercing of the ornamental bands with auger holes takes its place with the work found in the Read house.

There are a number of other interesting houses along the few streets of New Castle which are similar to those shown here. Fortunately there seems a good chance that they will remain for some time to come, for not only is industry removed but in this older town there is a compactness, with the houses built as close to one another as in a city on plots of narrow frontage, which will keep the newcomer from squeezing in as he has on the larger plots of many of the New England towns.

There is, moreover, another reason for the probable permanence of the town as it now stands, in that there is a real pride and understanding in the community of the architectural heritage represented by these buildings, an appreciation of tradition which is in restful contrast to the incessant changes which are sweeping away so much of our colonial background. New Castle is still the complete setting for the simple and genteel life which brought these eighteenth-century houses into existence.

LIVING ROOM MANTEL—THE VAN DYCK HOUSE, NEW CASTLE, DELAWARE

THE CHARLES THOMAS HOUSE, NEW CASTLE, DELAWARE
(Built about 1801—*Now called "The Parish House")*

THE KENSEY
JOHNS HOUSE

NEW CASTLE, DELAWARE

❦

MEASURED DRAWINGS *from*
The George F. Lindsay Collection

❦

MAIN STAIRS

PANELLING
AND MANTEL
IN THE
DINING ROOM

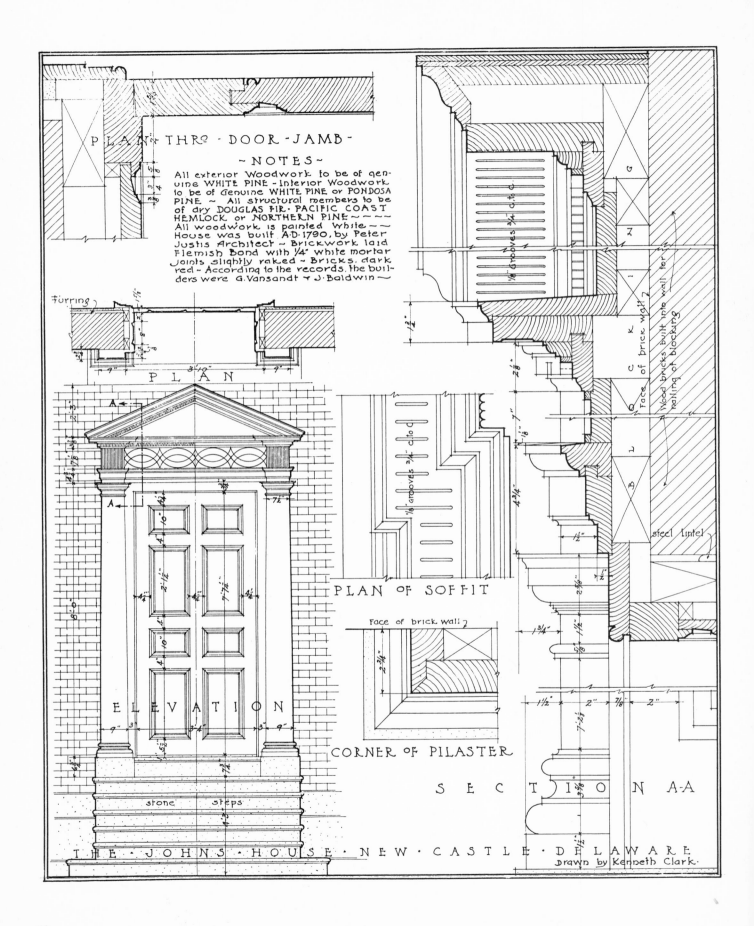

PLAN · THRO · DOOR · JAMB ·

~ NOTES ~

All exterior Woodwork to be of genuine WHITE PINE - Interior Woodwork
to be of Genuine WHITE PINE or PONDOSA
PINE ~ All structural members to be
of dry DOUGLAS FIR · PACIFIC COAST
HEMLOCK or NORTHERN PINE ~ ~ ~
All woodwork is painted white ~ ~
House was built A·D·1790, by Peter
Justis Architect ~ Brickwork laid
Flemish Bond with 1/4" white mortar
joints slightly raked ~ Bricks, dark
red ~ According to the records, the builders were G. Vansandt + J. Baldwin ~

Furring

P L A N

PLAN OF SOFFIT

Face of brick wall

CORNER OF PILASTER

E L E V A T I O N

stone   steps

S E C T I O N   A·A

steel lintel

THE · JOHNS · HOUSE · NEW · CASTLE · DELAWARE
Drawn by Kenneth Clark.

60

THE KENSEY JOHNS HOUSE,
NEW CASTLE, DELAWARE

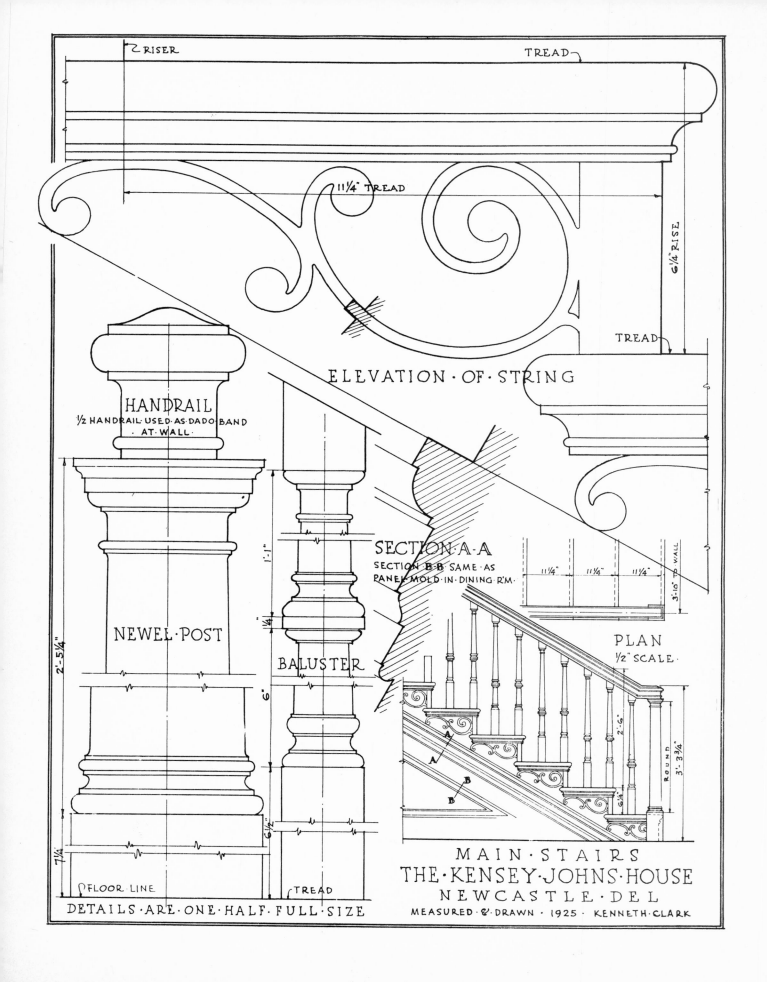

RISER — TREAD —

11¼" TREAD

6¼" RISE

TREAD

ELEVATION · OF · STRING

HANDRAIL
½ HANDRAIL · USED · AS · DADO · BAND
AT · WALL

NEWEL · POST

2'-5¼"

7¼"

FLOOR · LINE

BALUSTER

1'-1"

¼

6"

6½"

TREAD

SECTION · A · A
SECTION · B · B · SAME · AS
PANEL · MOLD · IN · DINING · R'M.

11¼" 11¼" 11¼"

3'-10" TO WALL

PLAN
½" SCALE

2'-6"

ROUND 3'-3¾"

6¼

A

B

B

DETAILS · ARE · ONE · HALF · FULL · SIZE

MAIN · STAIRS
THE · KENSEY · JOHNS · HOUSE
NEWCASTLE · DEL
MEASURED · & · DRAWN · 1925 · KENNETH · CLARK

DETAIL OF LIVING ROOM MANTEL

LIVING ROOM MANTEL

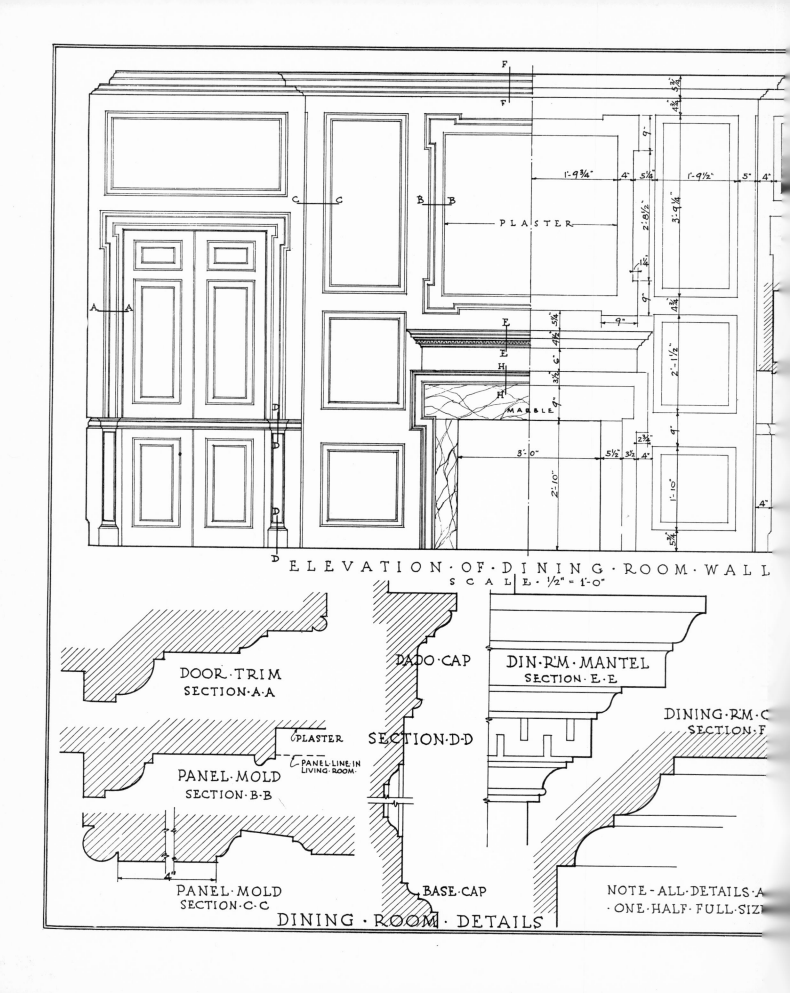

PLASTER

3¾
4¾
9"
1'-9¾" 4" 5¼ 1'-9½" 5" 4"
2'-8½"
1¼"
9"
4¾
5¼
4½" 4"
9"
3'-9¼"
2'-1½"
3½ 6"
9"
MARBLE
2¾
3'-0" 5½ 3½ 4"
1'-10"
9"
2'-10"
5¾
4"

ELEVATION·OF·DINING·ROOM·WALL

SCALE·½"=1'-0"

DOOR·TRIM
SECTION·A·A

PLASTER
PANEL·LINE·IN
LIVING·ROOM·

PANEL·MOLD
SECTION·B·B

4"

PANEL·MOLD
SECTION·C·C

DADO·CAP

SECTION·D·D

BASE·CAP

DIN·R'M·MANTEL
SECTION·E·E

DINING·R'M·C
SECTION·F

NOTE – ALL·DETAILS·A
·ONE·HALF·FULL·SIZE

DINING·ROOM·DETAILS

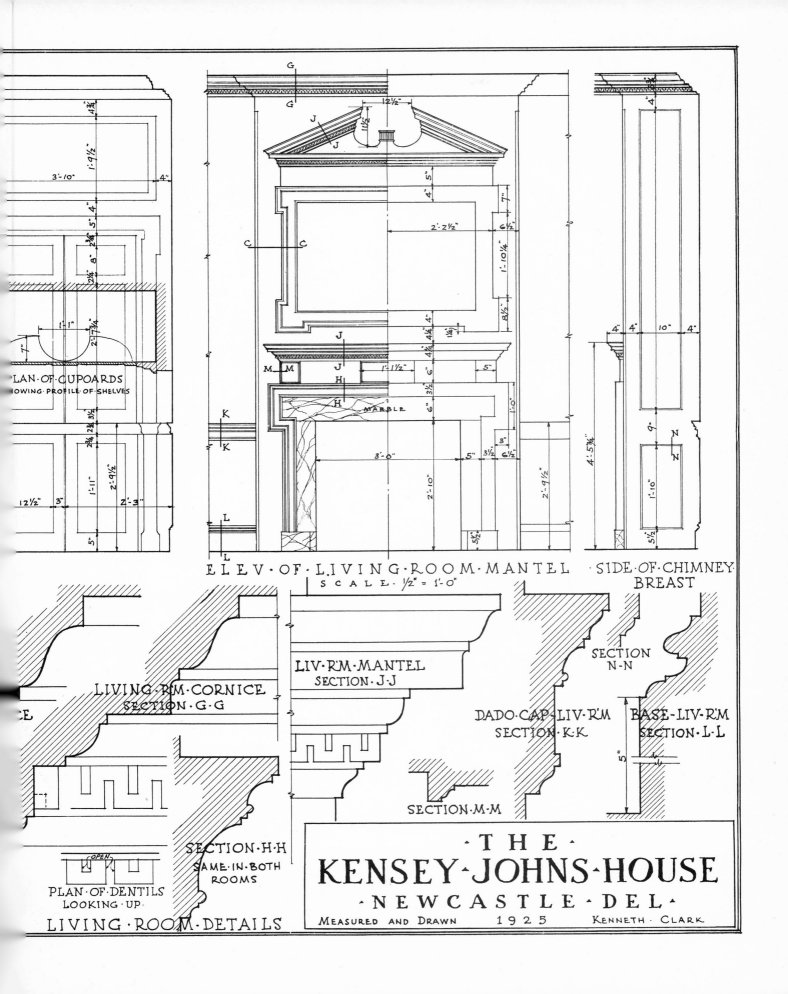

PLAN·OF·CUPOARDS
SHOWING·PROFILE·OF·SHELVES

MARBLE

ELEV·OF·LIVING·ROOM·MANTEL
SCALE·½" = 1'-0"

SIDE·OF·CHIMNEY
BREAST

LIVING·RM·CORNICE
SECTION·G·G

LIV·RM·MANTEL
SECTION·J·J

SECTION
N·N

DADO·CAP·LIV·RM
SECTION·K·K

BASE·LIV·RM
SECTION·L·L

SECTION·M·M

SECTION·H·H
SAME·IN·BOTH
ROOMS

OPEN

PLAN·OF·DENTILS
LOOKING·UP

LIVING·ROOM·DETAILS

·THE·
KENSEY·JOHNS·HOUSE
·NEWCASTLE·DEL·
MEASURED·AND·DRAWN   1925   KENNETH·CLARK

DOORWAY BETWEEN RECEPTION
AND LIVING ROOMS

MANTEL IN RECEPTION ROOM

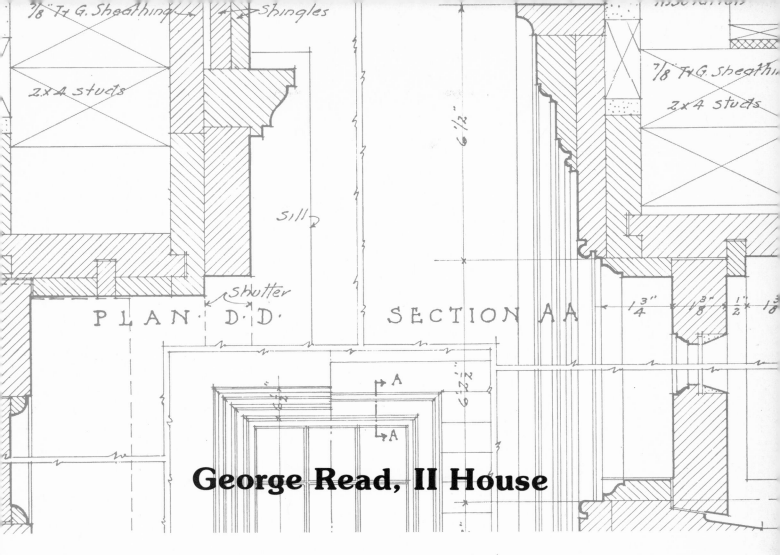

George Read, II House

WHEN the Swedish ships under the command of Peter Minuit anchored in the Delaware in 1638 their company of families bought from the Indians tracts which included the present sites of Wilmington and New Castle, and New Sweden was founded. The soil was fertile, game was abundant, and the settlement prospered. Even the arrival of Peter Stuyvesant in 1651 to claim the territory for the Dutch,—erecting Fort Casimir by way of emphasis,— and his naming the village New Amstel failed to shake the fortunes of the Swedes, for their individual holdings of land were not disturbed and they were allowed to continue their peaceful pursuits.

New Amstel was described as "a goodly town of about one hundred houses and containing a magazine, a guard house, a bake house and forge and residences for the clergymen and other officers." The settlement again fell into the hands of the Swedes and was again recovered by the Dutch; but upon Penn's arrival in 1682, he claimed the territory as a part of his Pennsylvania grant from the Duke of York, and thus terminated for all time the Swedish and Dutch authority upon the Delaware shores.

The town hall, the remains of the public market and, of course, the church and the court house can still be

seen, as well as a number of delightful old residences. Of these may be mentioned the "Amstel" House, the Kensey Johns House, the Van Dyke House, the Church (or Thomas) House, but the largest and finest residence of the town is the Read House, pictures of which are to be found on these pages.

The house was commenced by George Read, II, in 1791 and completed in 1801. The mansion of his father, the first George Read, who was a signer of the Declaration of Independence, stood to the south (or left) of the present Read House in what is now the garden, and fronted on "The Strand," as the street nearest the River is called. This house was destroyed by what the townsfolk call "The Great Fire" that swept New Castle in 1824 and destroyed some of the finest buildings.

The present mansion, erected by the son, occupies the northeast corner of a plot of ground having a frontage of about 180 feet on The Strand. The depth of the property is about 312 feet and extends to The Green. The walls are of brick, and it would be natural to suppose these were made at the southern end of the town long known as "Brickmaker's Point,"—where roofing tiles were also made,—if indeed the family records did not prove that they had been bought of Jeremiah Hornkett, brickmaker of Philadelphia, and transported

DETAIL OF PALLADIAN WINDOW

DETAIL OF FRONT DOORWAY

DETAIL OF DORMER

69

down the river by shallop at the rate of one dollar per thousand. The bricks are of a uniform rich dark red like the traditional Philadelphia "stretchers." They measure 8½ x 2 x 4¼ inches which approaches the standard brick of this country rather than the shorter and higher bricks imported from England. Thomas Spikeman of Wilmington laid the bricks. James Traquair of Philadelphia was the stonecutter. The lumber was also bought in Philadelphia, and Peter Crowding of that city was the contractor for the carpenter work.

A plot of well kept lawn stretches before the house and gives a broad outlook on the River. This space also gives a satisfactory view of the stately facade, distinguished as it is by the simplicity of parts characteristic of the English Georgian style, the finely wrought wood detail of the entrance, the Palladian window and the main cornice, the dormers of a form that rings tradi-

tionally true, and above all the balustrade enclosing a "Captain's Walk." Examining the facade in detail, it is found to be 49 feet 2 inches in width. Granite steps and platform lead to the front entrance with its doorway 4 feet 5 inches wide. Together with side lights and fluted pilasters of wood, the entrance measures 9 feet wide over all. An unusual device is to be seen in the divisions between the door and the side-lights. These are brought out to the face of the wall, thus recessing the door, as well as the side-lights, within deep panelled jambs and head of wood. The first story windows are 4 feet 3 inches wide; and as the bricks are so laid that five courses occupy 12¾ inches in height, the number of courses forming the jambs of the windows can be counted and the height of 8 feet 3½ inches ascertained. The marble window heads are really lintels with joint lines incised upon them to give the semblance of vous-

THE GEORGE
READ, II HOUSE,
NEW CASTLE,
DELAWARE

DETAIL OF FRONT—THE GEORGE READ, II HOUSE

Detail of "Second Floor Drawing Room"

DETAIL, HALL

HALL—THE GEORGE READ, II HOUSE, NEW CASTLE, DELAWARE

soirs. The ironwork appears to be of later date than that of the house itself.

The depth of the main or front body of the house is 46 feet 8 inches. A hallway 8 or 9 feet wide traverses the center of the house from the front entrance to the rear doorway opening upon the garden. The parlour and library divide equally the space upon the left of the hall. That upon the right is occupied by a square stair hall at the center, in front of which is the dining room and behind is the breakfast room. Beyond the last named and extending 50 feet or so further to the rear is the kitchen and service wing.

The interior doorways are provided with pilasters and entablatures in carved wood. With apologies to the editor of a journal once devoted to white pine, we remark that the doors themselves are of mahogany. Their surrounding detail is of pine, however, and bears many coats of white paint. The design is derived from classic forms but here used with a freedom leading to an effect a modern architect might yearn in vain to realize, daring not to depart from his books. Should he do so his innovations would be adjudged unpardonable. Yet similar crudities are present here and criticism is stilled. The reason? Time has consecrated them. Then, too, the touch of the hand everywhere noticeable on these mouldings of long ago has laid upon them a pliancy and softness which dwell not in the products of modern planing mills and machinery.

In the frieze and centerpiece of a mantel "French putty" ornaments are found depicting a gentleman-at-arms being driven in a lion chariot, preceded by a flying messenger and followed by his armed retainers. Architraves, skirting and chair rails have generous proportions and heavy projections. The ornament and decoration of the woodwork continue through the first floor. In the library it is as elaborate as in the parlour. The dining room is simpler, with a mantel from which all the moulding decoration is omitted; but the stairway

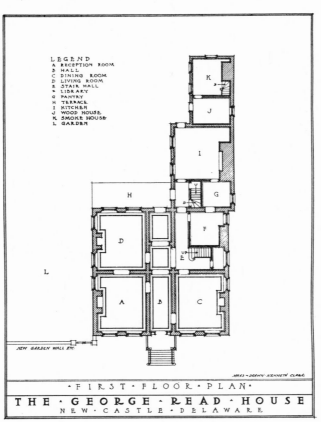

LEGEND
A RECEPTION ROOM
B HALL
C DINING ROOM
D LIVING ROOM
E STAIR HALL
F LIBRARY
G PANTRY
H TERRACE
I KITCHEN
J WOOD HOUSE
K SMOKE HOUSE
L GARDEN

NEW GARDEN WALL ETC.

MEAS. DRAWN KENNETH CLARK

· F I R S T · F L O O R · P L A N ·

THE · GEORGE · READ · HOUSE
NEW · CASTLE · DELAWARE

and the second story hall are similar in treatment to the elaborate rooms of the first floor, yet they are quite distinct in detail. On the second floor, too, is the drawing room which is quite the most elaborate room of all and again displays distinct differences of detail. A fine ornamental frieze in moulded plaster is an added touch of decoration which distinguishes this room.

The hardware throughout the main part of the house is quite original, the escutcheons being formed of interlaced silver strands half round in section. In one of the second floor bedrooms there is a quaint arrangement of wires running through pulleys permitting the brass bolt of the door to be opened by a person lying in bed.

Upon entering the house, if the weather be warm, one sees the garden beyond through a doorway elaborated with pilasters and semi-circular transom with fan light, and over all a horizontal cornice. Here is a brick-paved space under a grape arbor, and beyond them are greenhouse, potting house and tool house.

The garden was laid out in 1846 by Robert Buist. Its front portion, extending about 130 feet along The Strand and equaling the depth of the house, is laid out in three geometric parterres. Beyond this is the portion laid out in serpentine paths between cedar trees, box bushes, balsam firs and a great maple. Further on is the kitchen garden where at two corners stand English walnut trees. An aged Balm of Gilead, a magnolia macrophylla and a crepe myrtle are treasured landmarks.

In 1845 the property was bought by the Couper Family, of which a descendent, Miss Hettie Smith, was long the owner and occupant. Fortunately, the present owner, Mr. Philip Laird, is not only sensible of the architectural treasure in his keeping, but delights in its possession. Upon acquiring it he had it restored as far as possible to its original condition. This work was done under the intelligent and sympathetic direction of Brown and Whiteside, Architects of Wilmington, who also added the brick wall surrounding the garden and the gateway.

Detail of Doorway, Second Story Hall

Detail of Stairway at First Floor level

Reception Room of

THE GEORGE READ, II HOUSE

NEW CASTLE, DELAWARE

MEASURED DRAWINGS *from*
The George F. Lindsay Collection

*Detail of Doorway between
Reception and Living Rooms*

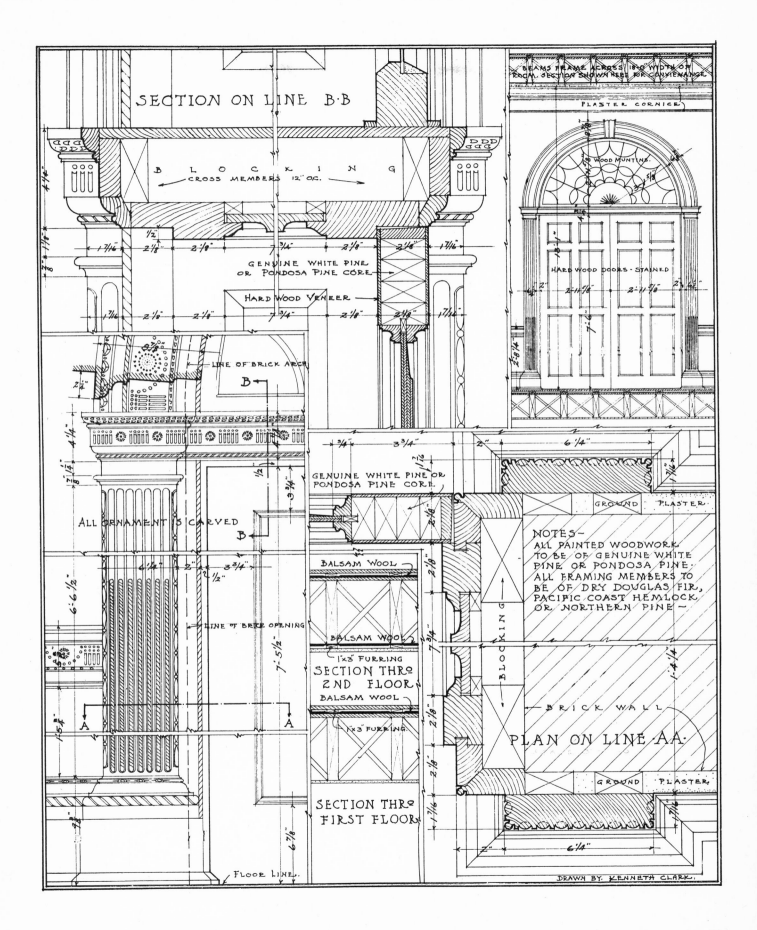

SECTION ON LINE B·B

BLOCKING
← CROSS MEMBERS 12" O.C. →

GENUINE WHITE PINE
OR PONDOSA PINE CORE

HARD WOOD VENEER

LINE OF BRICK ARCH

B

B

ALL ORNAMENT IS CARVED

LINE OF BRICK OPENING

A   A

FLOOR LINE

GENUINE WHITE PINE OR
PONDOSA PINE CORE

BALSAM WOOL

BALSAM WOOL

1x3 FURRING

SECTION THR°
2ND FLOOR

BALSAM WOOL

1x3 FURRING

SECTION THR°
FIRST FLOOR

BEAMS FRAME ACROSS 18'-0 WIDTH OF
ROOM. SECTION SHOWN HERE FOR CONVIENANCE

PLASTER CORNICE

WOOD MUNTINS

HARD WOOD DOORS - STAINED

GROUND   PLASTER

BLOCKING

NOTES -
ALL PAINTED WOODWORK
TO BE OF GENUINE WHITE
PINE OR PONDOSA PINE
ALL FRAMING MEMBERS TO
BE OF DRY DOUGLAS FIR,
PACIFIC COAST HEMLOCK
OR NORTHERN PINE ~

BRICK WALL

PLAN ON LINE AA·

GROUND   PLASTER

DRAWN BY. KENNETH CLARK.

77

DETAIL, A—MANTEL—THE GEORGE READ, II HOUSE, NEW CASTLE, DELAWARE

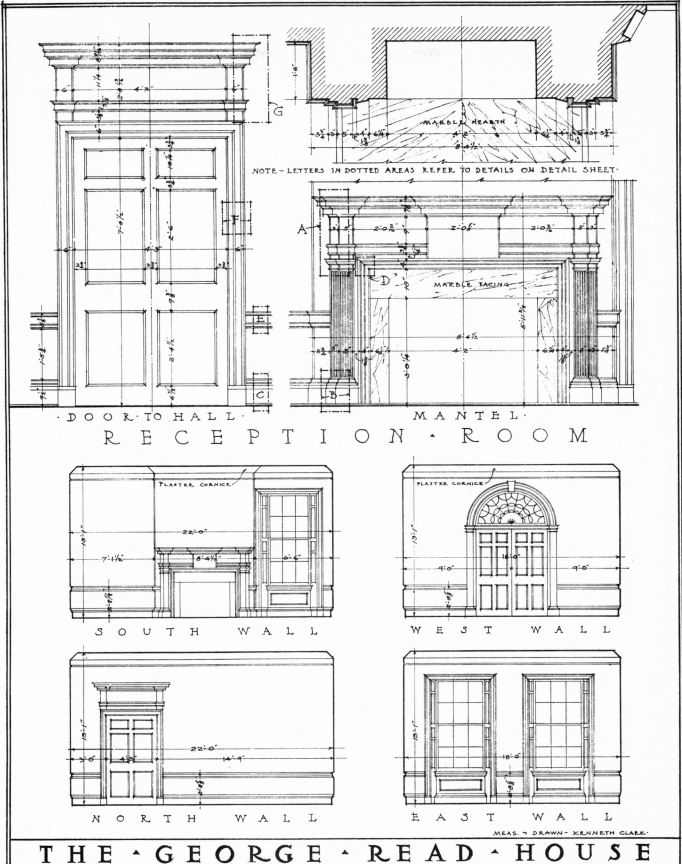

NOTE – LETTERS IN DOTTED AREAS REFER TO DETAILS ON DETAIL SHEET.

MARBLE HEARTH

MARBLE FACING

· D O O R · T O · H A L L ·   · M A N T E L ·

R E C E P T I O N · R O O M

PLASTER CORNICE

PLASTER CORNICE

· S O U T H · W A L L ·   · W E S T · W A L L ·

· N O R T H · W A L L ·   · E A S T · W A L L ·

MEAS. & DRAWN – KENNETH CLARK

T H E · G E O R G E · R E A D · H O U S E
N E W · C A S T L E · D E L A W A R E ·

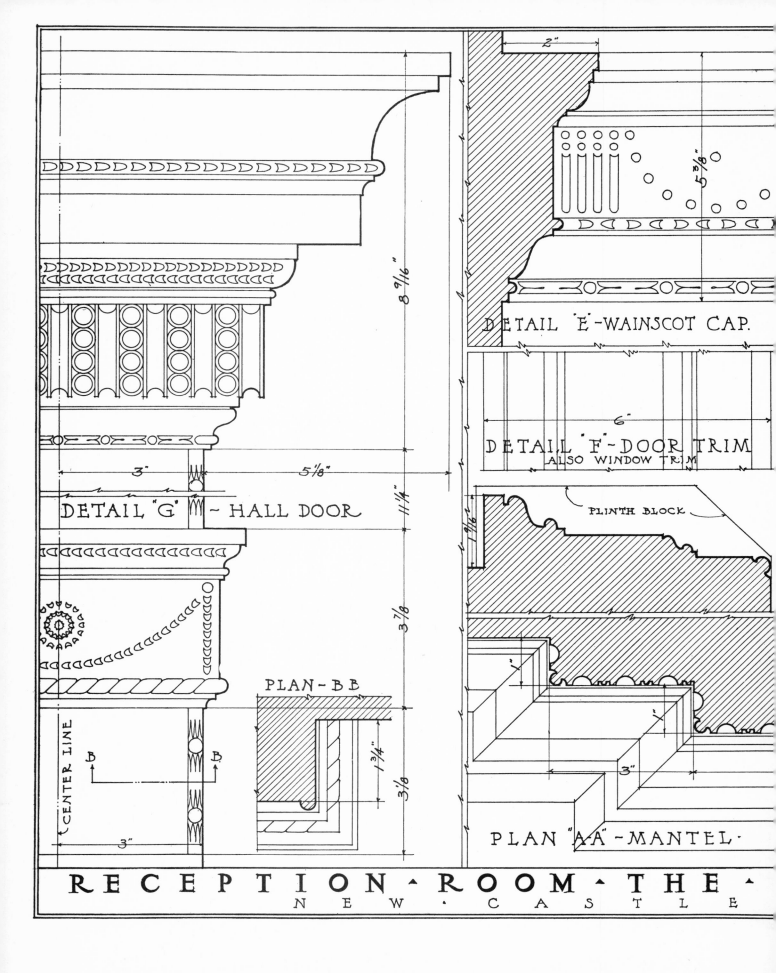

2"

DETAIL "E"-WAINSCOT CAP.

8 9/16"

DETAIL "F"-DOOR TRIM
ALSO WINDOW TRIM

PLINTH BLOCK

3"

5/8"

DETAIL "G" ~ HALL DOOR

11/4"

3/8"

PLAN · BB

1 3/4"

3/8"

CENTER LINE

B   B

3"

PLAN "AA"-MANTEL·

3"

RECEPTION · ROOM · THE ·

NEW · CASTLE

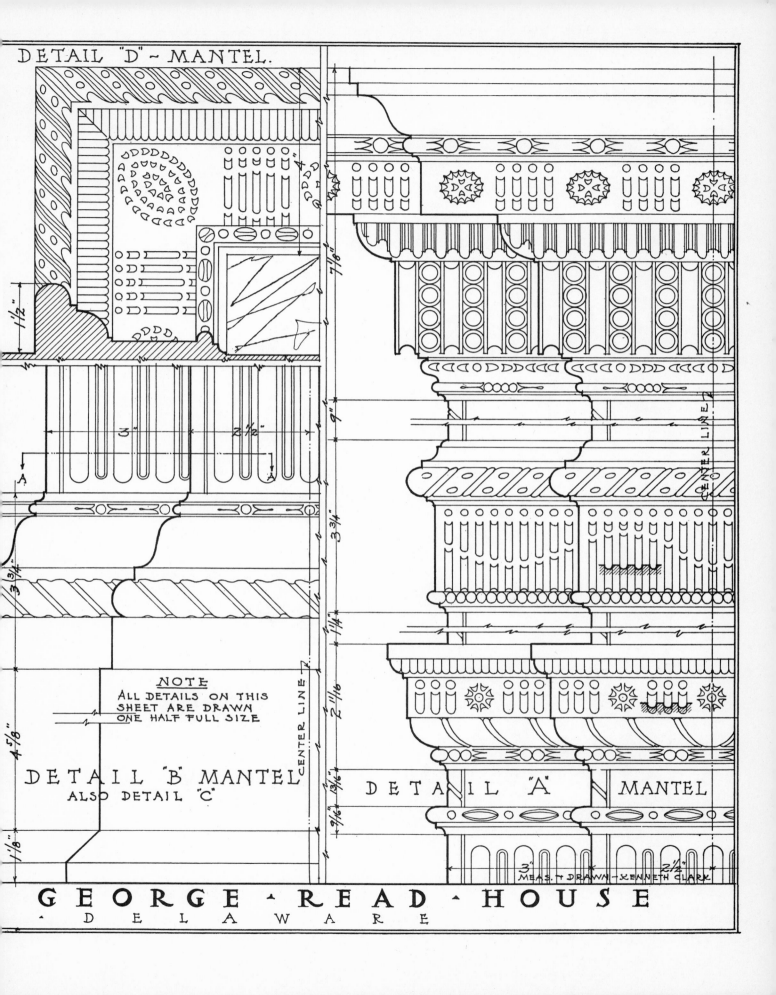

DETAIL "D" ~ MANTEL.

1½"

4"

NOTE
ALL DETAILS ON THIS
SHEET ARE DRAWN
ONE HALF FULL SIZE

3"   2½"

A   A

3¾"

4⅝"

1⅛"

DETAIL "B" MANTEL
ALSO DETAIL "C"

CENTER LINE

7⅛"

9"

3¾"

1¼"

2 11/16"

13/16"

9/16"

CENTER LINE 2

DETAIL "A" MANTEL

3"   2½"
MEAS. + DRAWN ~ KENNETH CLARK

GEORGE · READ · HOUSE
· D E L A W A R E ·

THE SMALLWOOD—JONES HOUSE, NEW BERN, NORTH CAROLINA

A North Carolina Townhouse

THE Smallwood-Jones House at New Bern, North Carolina, is a survival of a prosperous period in the early days of that community. Built by an architect and a builder of whom research does not reveal the names it is an excellent example of what the well-to-do merchant of that place and time considered to be the proper thing for himself and family. It is a small house, the entire original building being enclosed with a space of 36x40 feet, but the interior gives an impression of spaciousness and stateliness which belie the actual dimensions. Facing on East Front Street, with its rear overlooking a long grassy vista sloping to the banks of the River Nuse, it has seen the coming and passing of many generations, and survived the vicissitudes of fire, flood and war. It has been tenderly cared for through succeeding generations and is today in the hands of sympathetic and appreciative people who are restoring

it and placing it in condition to survive the coming years, that posterity may see, admire and reflect.

The front elevation presents to the street a simple, reserved aspect with components beautifully spaced in a richly textured wall of common brick. The bonding is Flemish and the brick joints, of gray mortar, are about 3/8 of an inch wide and struck flush with the surface. Both brick and mortar have weathered until they have reached the point which gives these old brick walls the quality that accounts for much of their charm; so difficult to reproduce in new work. The spacing of openings is symmetrical except for the dormers which do not center over the windows below. The main cornice, the porch and the dormer pediments are lavishly decorated with hand carved ornament. Because New England has always been extolled as the source of nicely executed detail, etc., while the South has been considered as lacking the proper craftsmen, it is hard to realize that the

FRONT PORCH—THE SMALLWOOD—JONES HOUSE, NEW BERN, NORTH CAROLINA

THE SMALLWOOD—JONES HOUSE, NEW BERN, NORTH CAROLINA

ornamental work on the Smallwood-Jones house was done locally. However, there is every reason to believe that the carving was done here and it ranks with the best of the old work irrespective of time and place.

The detail, molding systems and other individual parts of the cornices, etc., are decidedly original in design and placing and, where most of the New England detail can be assigned to a definite inspirational source, such as Langly, Paine, or other authorities of the period, this work has an originality and freshness that is individual to it and the similar houses of this town. There is a very indefinitely founded tradition in New Bern that these houses were done by one James Coor, a naval architect or builder of ships who came there in 1800 to practice his profession and turned his talents to architecture. Such a tradition might account for some of the unorthodox detail, which, with the use of the rope molding so consistently, has a decidedly "shippy" look.

The ugly block which terminates the porch capitols is a repair, the originals similar to the pilaster caps. The roof was originally shingled, but was replaced at a later day by one of the less sympathetic standing seam tin. With the exception of the few changes mentioned, the exterior presents its original appearance.

The plan is unusual in that it has a hall 11′ 2″ wide at the right side running through the house with a door in the rear wall and another at the side. This seems at first glance an uneconomical feature, but in reality this hall forms a second living room, well ventilated from three exposures, and in the warm summer must be a comfortable and practical room. To the left of this hall as one enters is the room known as the "Counting Room" which a former owner set aside as an office and which was at one time entered direct from the street by the cutting down of the left hand window of the elevation to form a door; this was probably done long after the house was built and it has since been filled in and the elevation restored to its original appearance. The Counting room has a fine mantel to which has been added an overmantel treatment that does not agree in scale with the original. Back of the Counting room and also opening off the hall at the right, is the dining room, with a cornice that caps the room with a real feeling of scale. The relation in size of the cornice and its members to those of the overmantel cornice and the pediment just below is a remarkable example of judgment of scale on the part of the designer meriting serious consideration, for were one or the other too large or too small by the smallest amount the scale of the entire room would suffer. The relation is, however, perfect and contributes in no small measure to the "handsomeness" and dignity of the whole. The service to the dining room was originally from the basement, which accounts in part for the modern addition of kitchen, pantry, etc., at the rear.

The second floor is unique in that it has the formal drawing room necessitated by the use of the usual first floor space for the Counting room. In this second floor drawing room, we see the genius of the architect and the skill of his craftsmen, who executed the work, at their best. Here was lavished all they knew of decoration in its architectural sense. All the old gagets, dentils, ropes, frets, wave motives, interlacement bands and carved sunbursts are here, but all are used in their proper place, so well designed and scaled that each goes to make up the ensemble without intruding its individuality. The ornament is of carved wood, the work of a master craftsman; the rope moldings are cut in the round and applied; the fret and the interlacement band are jig-sawed out of $\frac{3}{16}$″ stuff and nailed on with hand made nails, of which there is hardly an evidence on the surface. The panelling has the molds cut on the stiles and the panel set in solid without a back mold. All is dovetailed and dowelled together in the manner of the ancient cabinetmaker who had the time and the inclination to do things right, once, and for all time. There is a new door in this room which was added to the East wall in modern times and though the workmen tried to copy the old work exactly the "Touch" is not there. Even on close examination, it is difficult to point out any apparent variation, but the whole thing has a different look. The craftsman has been succeeded by the mechanic, the artist by the plane pusher.

To the east of the Drawing room is a small room, perhaps originally a library, with the same trim and embellishments as the former. There is some evidence that this was at one time part of the drawing room, making one long room entirely across the front of the house, but it seems hard to account for this in plan if the window on the East elevation which has been moved, was formerly on axis.

The entire house, inside and out, shows a careful, studied solution of a domestic architectural problem that the modern architect may study with profit. As an inspiration in designing a modern American house, it is certainly more fitting than the Italian, Spanish and other foreign styles that have been "the thing" lately. American architecture has an indigenous background that deserves more consideration at the hands of her architects than it is given. If the young American, whose steps are on the brink of an architectural career, would take heed to the slogan "See America First", our homes would begin to reflect our ancestry and not the "Melting Pot".

THE SMALLWOOD—JONES HOUSE, NEW BERN, NORTH CAROLINA

THE SMALLWOOD—JONES HOUSE, NEW BERN, NORTH CAROLINA

THE SMALLWOOD—JONES HOUSE, NEW BERN, NORTH CAROLINA

THE SMALLWOOD—JONES HOUSE, NEW BERN, NORTH CAROLINA

The SMALLWOOD·JONES HOUSE
NEW BERN, NORTH CAROLINA

MEASURED DRAWINGS *from*
The George F. Lindsay Collection

SECOND FLOOR DRAWING ROOM—THE SMALLWOOD—JONES HOUSE, NEW BERN, NORTH CAROLINA

FIRST FLOOR HALL—THE SMALLWOOD—JONES HOUSE, NEW BERN, NORTH CAROLINA

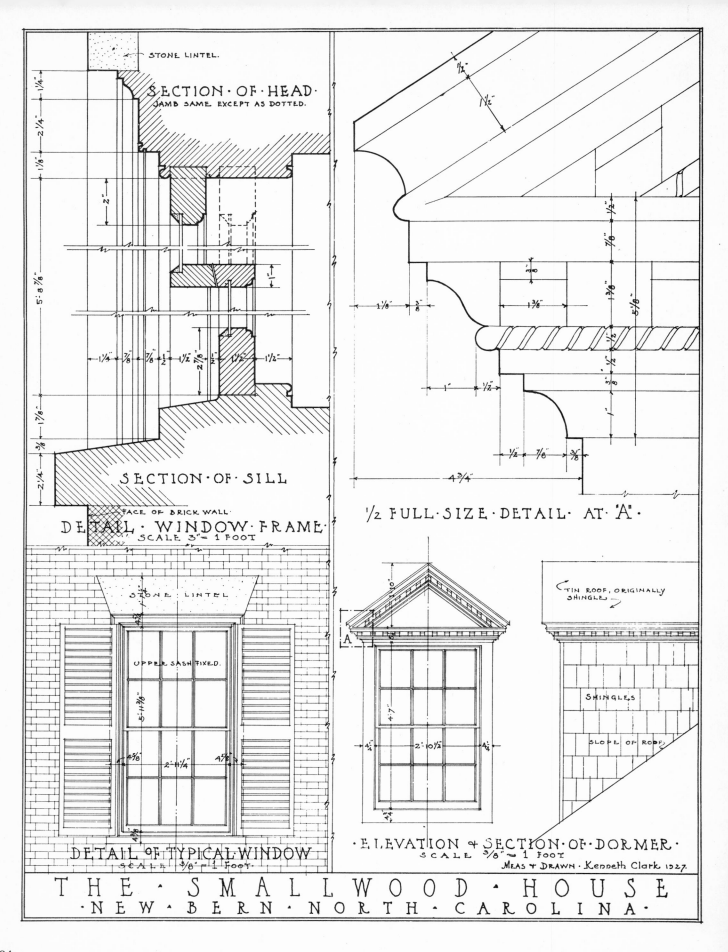

STONE LINTEL.

SECTION·OF·HEAD·
JAMB SAME EXCEPT AS DOTTED.

SECTION·OF·SILL

FACE OF BRICK WALL

DETAIL·WINDOW·FRAME·
SCALE 3" = 1 FOOT

½ FULL·SIZE·DETAIL·AT·'A'·

STONE LINTEL

UPPER SASH FIXED.

DETAIL OF TYPICAL WINDOW
SCALE 3/8" = 1 FOOT

TIN ROOF, ORIGINALLY SHINGLE

SHINGLES

SLOPE OF ROOF

·ELEVATION & SECTION·OF·DORMER·
SCALE 3/8" = 1 FOOT

MEAS & DRAWN · Kenneth Clark · 1927.

THE · SMALLWOOD · HOUSE
·NEW · BERN · NORTH · CAROLINA·

THE SMALLWOOD—JONES HOUSE, NEW BERN, NORTH CAROLINA

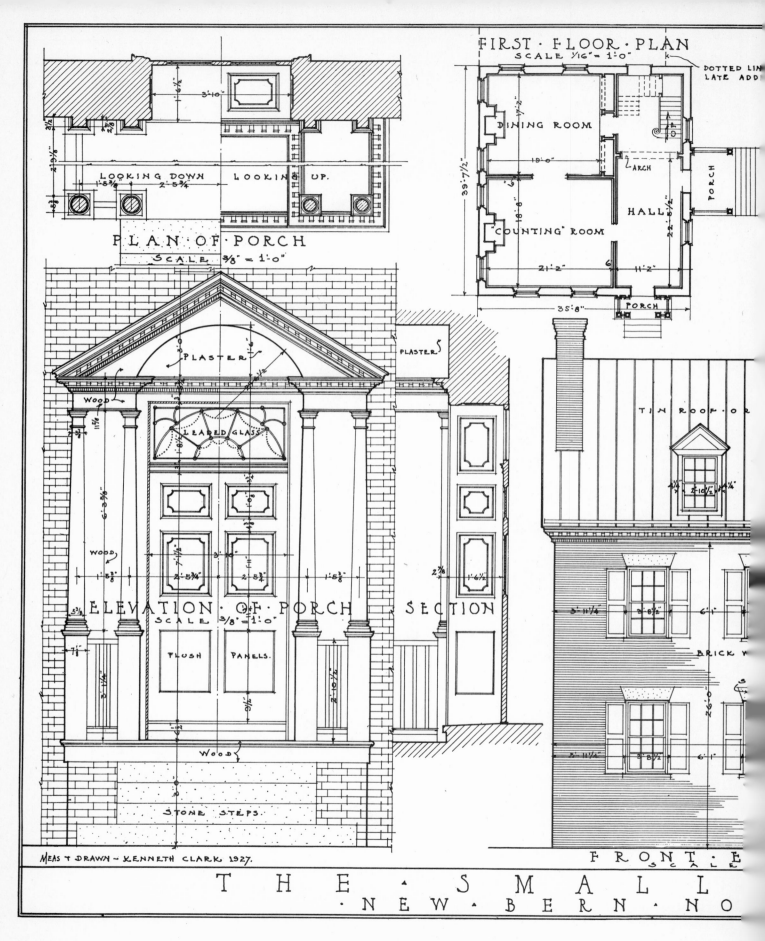

FIRST · FLOOR · PLAN
SCALE 1/16" = 1'0"

DOTTED LIN[E]
LATE ADD[ITION]

DINING ROOM

"COUNTING" ROOM

HALL

ARCH

PORCH

PORCH

LOOKING DOWN   LOOKIN[G] UP.

PLAN OF PORCH
SCALE 3/8" = 1'0"

PLASTER

PLASTER

WOOD

LEADED GLASS

WOOD

ELEVATION · OF · PORCH   SECTION
SCALE 3/8" = 1'0"

FLUSH   PANELS.

WOOD

STONE STEPS

TIN · ROOF · O[R]

BRICK [W]

MEAS.T DRAWN ~ KENNETH CLARK 1927.

FRONT · E[LEVATION]
SCALE

THE · SMALL
· NEW · BERN · NO[RTH]

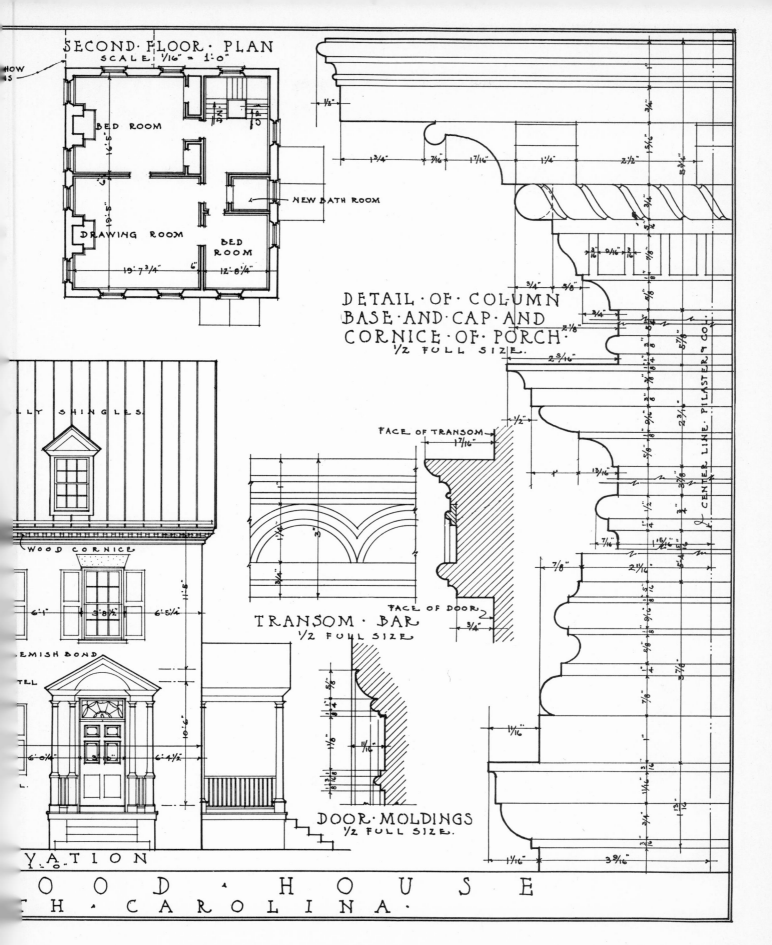

SECOND · FLOOR · PLAN
SCALE: 1/16" = 1'-0"

BED ROOM

NEW BATH ROOM

DRAWING ROOM

BED ROOM

19'·7 3/4"

12'·8 1/4"

DETAIL · OF · COLUMN
BASE · AND · CAP · AND
CORNICE · OF · PORCH·
1/2 FULL SIZE.

SHINGLES.

WOOD · CORNICE

FLEMISH BOND

FACE OF TRANSOM

FACE OF DOOR

TRANSOM · BAR
1/2 FULL SIZE.

DOOR · MOLDINGS
1/2 FULL SIZE.

C.L. CENTER LINE. PILASTER & CO.

YATION

OOD · HOUSE
TH · CAROLINA·

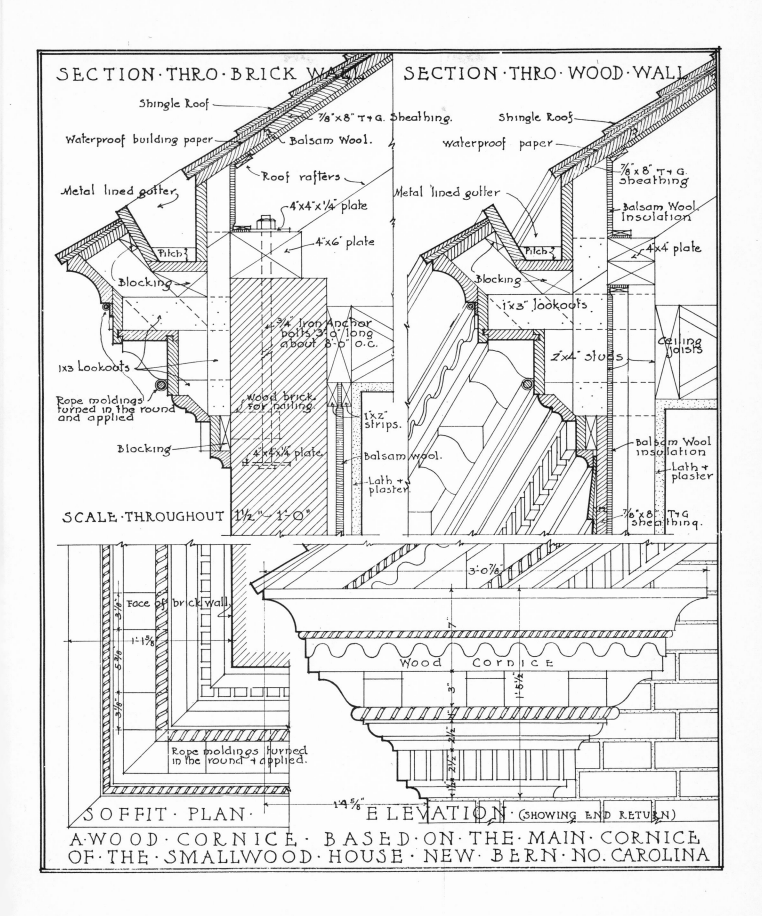

SECTION·THRO·BRICK WALL SECTION·THRO·WOOD·WALL

Shingle Roof
Waterproof building paper
⅞"x8" T+G. Sheathing.
Balsam Wool.
Roof rafters
Metal lined gutter
4"x4"x¼" plate
Pitch
4"x6" plate
Blocking
1x3 Lookouts
4¾" Iron Anchor bolts 3'-0" long about 8'-0" O.C.
Rope moldings turned in the round and applied
Wood brick for nailing.
Blocking
4"x4"x¼" plate

SCALE·THROUGHOUT 1½" = 1'-0"

1x2" strips.
Balsam wool.
Lath + plaster

Shingle Roof
Waterproof paper
⅞"x8" T+G. sheathing
Balsam Wool Insulation
Metal lined gutter
4x4 plate
Pitch
Blocking
1x3" lookouts
Ceiling joists
2"x4" studs
Balsam Wool insulation
Lath + plaster
⅞"x8" T+G sheathing.

Face of brick wall
3/8
1'-1⅝
5⅝
3/8
Rope moldings turned in the round + applied.

SOFFIT·PLAN·

3'-0⅞
Wood   Cornice
3
1'-5½
2½
2½
½
2½
1'-9⅝"

ELEVATION· (SHOWING END RETURN)

A·WOOD·CORNICE·BASED·ON·THE·MAIN·CORNICE·
OF·THE·SMALLWOOD·HOUSE·NEW·BERN·NO. CAROLINA

HOME MORAVIAN CHURCH (SALEM)
WINSTON-SALEM, NORTH CAROLINA

Erected 1800

Old Salem, North Carolina

Who settled this old town? Empire Builders! Let us take a tiny peep into the distant past for an historical background, and we will see a pageantry of war and persecution.

Attilla and his Huns destroying Bohemia about 800 A.D. Prince Mojmir building churches in Moravia, a province of Bohemia, in 836 A.D. John Huss, who was born in Bohemia in 1369. Gregory, the Patriarch. Formation of Unitas Fratrum, *The United Brethren*, now the Moravian Church, in 1457. Luke of Prague, born in 1460. Martin Luther! John Augusta, son of a hatter, born in Prague in 1500. The Brethren driven from Bohemia and Moravia. John Amos Commenius and Christan David, who led the Brethren to a refuge on the great wooded estate of Count Nicholas Louis von Zinzendorf located in Hurrnhut, Saxony. Under the patronage of Count Zinzendorf, we see their movement into Germany 1735-1775 and into England 1728-1775 and to America; their arrival in Georgia, under the leadership of Spangenberg, in 1735 and their movement to Pennsylvania 1740-1775.

Spangenberg, with a small band of men, left Bethlehem, Pennsylvania, November 29th, 1751 and located, in North Carolina, a tract of 100,000 acres granted the brethren by Lord Granville. Spangenberg completed his survey January 25th, 1753 and named the tract *Wachovia*. On October 8th, 1753, twelve single brethren set out from Bethlehem for Wachovia. This small group of men included a Pastor, warden, physician, tailor, baker, shoemaker, tanner, gardener and three farmers. They arrived on November 17th, to start the building of *Bethabra* known to us as "Old Town." About the Old Town church was constructed a fort to which, later on, came many other settlers for protection from Indians. The old fort has disappeared but a quiet little path still leads to God's Acre, or the burying ground, with its quaintly lettered soapstone markers, where rest many of these early Empire Builders. In 1756, the colony of Bethabra consisted of sixty-five souls.

It had always been the intention of these first settlers to establish a town near the center of their tract where greater activities could be undertaken. On February 14th, 1765, a site, eight miles south of Bethabra, was chosen and christened "Salem" by Count Zinzendorf.

Frederick William von Marshall took a very active part in the selection of the site. His resting place can be seen in the present awe inspiring God's Acre of Salem, the simple flat stone bearing the dates 1721-1802.

The Church at Bethabra was erected in 1788, the first Church of *Wachovia*. The charm of this building lies in simple design, rugged masonry, stone and wide pine plank floors, wide pine plank ceilings, simple detail and inspiring cupola. Truly, its designer was an artist! I wish the reader could see its barrel vaulted cellar, its roof framing connected with pins and the ingenuous method of supporting its cupola.

The Home Moravian Church is, like the Old Town Church, characterized by its beautiful stone and brick masonry, wonderful joinery, simple design and general dignity. The interior has been rebuilt, the plan having

THE OLD SALEM TAVERN (SALEM)
WINSTON-SALEM, NORTH CAROLINA

Erected 1784

Detail of Staircase, Erected 1784

THE CHRISTOPHER REICH HOUSE, ERECTED 1815
(SALEM) WINSTON-SALEM, NORTH CAROLINA

THE WACHOVIA HISTORICAL SOCIETY BUILDING (SALEM) WINSTON–SALEM, NORTH CAROLINA

Formerly the Salem Boys School, Erected 1794

CHURCH AT BETHABRA,
NOW KNOWN AS "OLD TOWN",
NORTH CAROLINA (1788)

been reversed and enlarged.

From the large stone platform in front of the entrance, on every Easter morning, before the sun has risen, the Venerable Bishop speaks a few simple words to the assembled multitude and the slow and solemn march starts on its journey of a few hundred yards to God's Acre, to the music of carols, accompanied by a band of several hundred instruments. Here the Bishop completes the simple service as the sun rises!

The Sisters House was erected in two units, the two doorways of the left being in the first unit. The point where the second unit was added is easily distinguished.

The cornerstone of the first unit was laid on March 31st, 1785 and was dedicated April 5th, 1786. For many years this building was the center of Womens' Activities in the community.

This old masterpiece is rich in its lovely crown of orange roof tile blended with black; its European suggestion in fenestration and dormers, brick masonry, hand wrought hardware, simple and dignified detail, perfect proportion, old whitewashed plaster and wide plank and stone floors scrubbed clean.

The outside walls, above grade, are constructed of extremely large hand made clay brick, 11 7/8" x 5" x 2 3/4", laid Flemish bond. We in modern times in laying up a wall of this character in Flemish bond would cut a brick to form a "closer" to fill the rectangle at the corners of alternate courses; not so these people. They molded and burned tiny clay bricks to fill these voids.

The present Office Building, Salem College, was erected in 1810 and was used as the residence of the first "Inspector" of Salem Female Academy. It carries an echo of the detail of the Sisters House. A stone vaulted cellar is an interesting feature.

The Brothers House, like the Sisters House, was erected in two units. The frame structure on the right was begun August 30th, 1768 and was dedicated December 27th, 1769. The brick addition to the left was added in 1786. The Brothers House was for many years the industrial center of the community. The street level in

CUPOLA OF HOME MORAVIAN CHURCH
FROM REAR OF OLD SALEM BOYS' SCHOOL
(SALEM) WINSTON-SALEM, NORTH CAROLINA

front of this building was originally much lower than at present, thus permitting cellar windows.

The construction of the frame unit of this building is unusual. Logs of large diameter being difficult to secure, without transporting them seven or eight miles, which was a long distance in those days, the walls of this building were constructed of logs of smaller diameter, erected *vertically* in two or more layers having their interstices filled with clay mixed with straw. The interior side of the walls was plastered; the exterior surfaces being covered with "clapboards," as we know them. This makes me think that possibly those who contend that this early outside covering was really known as "clayboards" are correct.

The Vogler House was erected in 1819 by John Vogler, a silversmith and expert cabinet maker.

The Salem Boys School was organized in 1777. The school building was begun May 1st, 1794 and occupied until 1896. It now shelters the collections of the Wachovia Historical Society.

In this old building, the first story walls are of stone, stuccoed, its details are similar to the Sisters House, an old oven and vaulting add interest to its interior. The principal feature of the interior is a continuous winding staircase, three stories in height, with details similar to the staircase in the Tavern.

The site for the Old Salem Tavern was selected in 1768. The first building was destroyed by fire January 31st, 1784. General George Washington was entertained in this hostelry May 31st, 1791.

All of Salem's ancient buildings are characterized by their simplicity and remarkable craftsmanship. Surely their builders must have been inspired. Nothing was wasted; everything was adequate.

These early builders founded an individual community which has grown to be a great city in a great state. We who know and love their purposes, ideals and hardships look upon their aesthetic accomplishments with awe!

ACADEMY STREET (SALEM)
WINSTON–SALEM, NORTH CAROLINIA

Looking from South Main Street to Church Street

Residence of First Inspector, Salem Female Academy, Salem

NOW OFFICE BUILDING, SALEM COLLEGE,
WINSTON–SALEM, NORTH CAROLINA

DETAIL: ENTRANCE

BISHOP'S HOUSE (SALEM) WINSTON-SALEM, NORTH CAROLINA
Erected 1841

MORAVIAN BROTHERS HOUSE (SALEM)
WINSTON-SALEM, NORTH CAROLINA

Erected 1768-1769

Entrance to Sisters House, Erected 1785-1786

MORAVIAN SISTERS HOUSE (SALEM)
WINSTON–SALEM, NORTH CAROLINA

Erected 1785-1786

THE JOHN VOGLER HOUSE—OLD SALEM
WINSTON-SALEM, NORTH CAROLINA

MEASURED DRAWINGS *from*
The George F. Lindsay Collection

THE JOHN VOGLER HOUSE (SALEM) WINSTON–SALEM, NORTH CAROLINA
Erected 1819

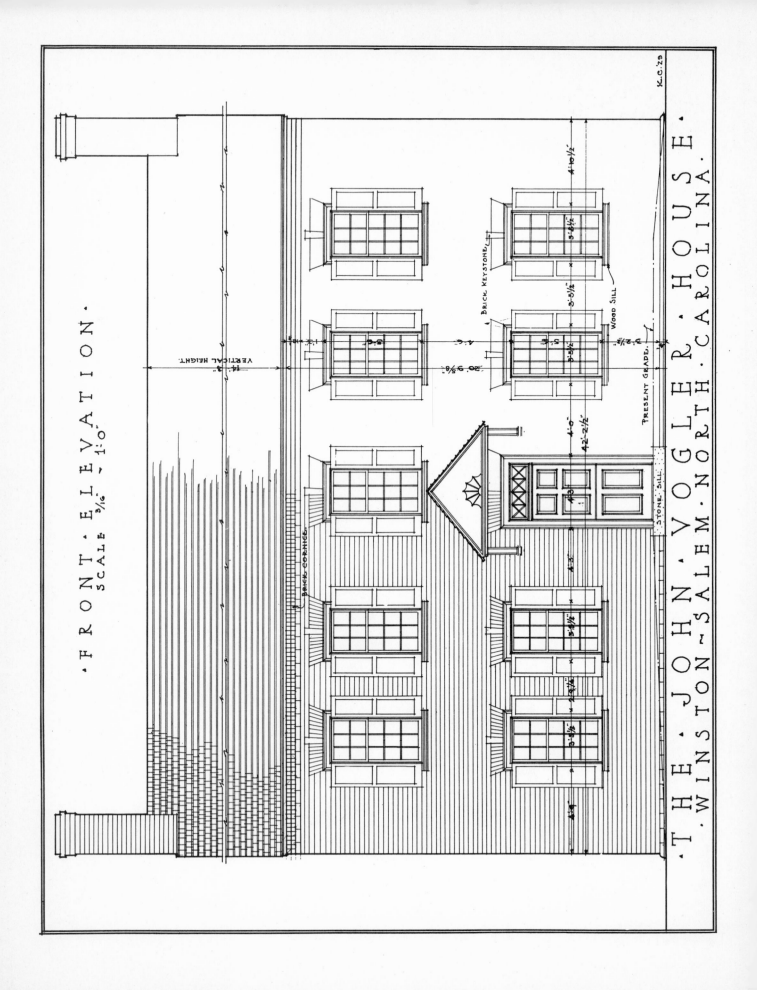

·FRONT·ELEVATION·
SCALE 3/16" = 1'·0"

·THE·JOHN·VOGLER·HOUSE·
·WINSTON~SALEM~NORTH·CAROLINA·

K.C.'29

DETAIL SHOWING ENTRANCE HOOD

SHINGLE ROOF

MATCHED BOARDS

GLASS

A   A

DUTCH DOOR

PRESENT GRADE

· SECTION ·   · DETAIL · OF · CENTRAL · PART · OF · FRONT ·
· T H E · J O H N · V O G L E R ·
· W I N S T O N · S A L E M · N O R T H · C A R O L I N A ·

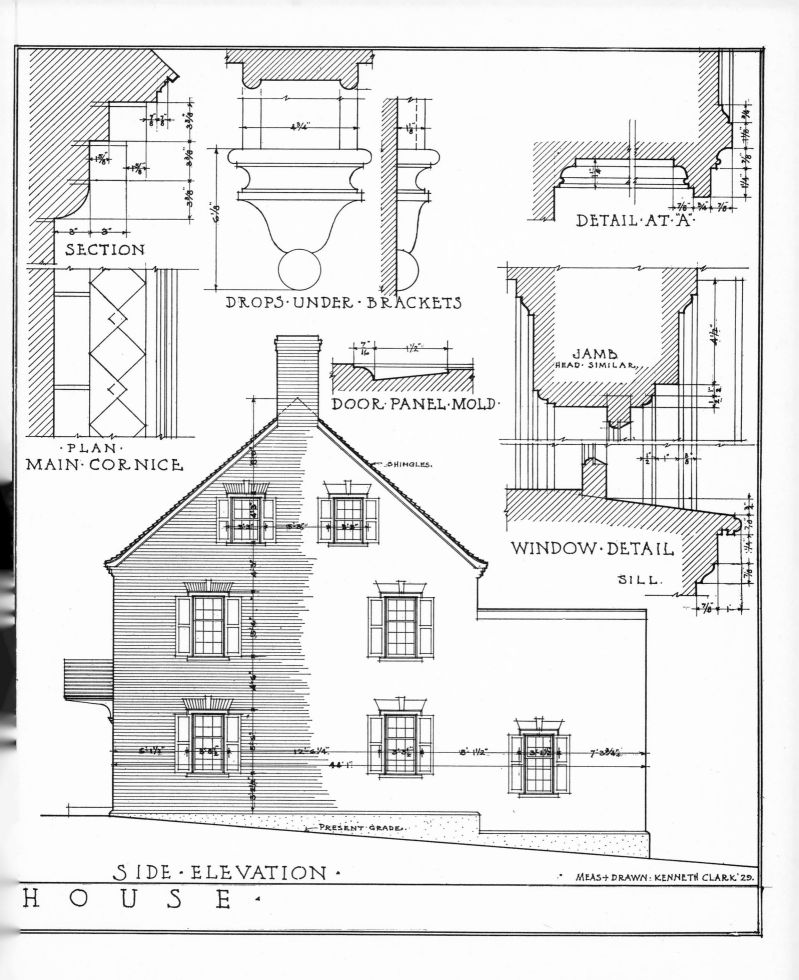

SECTION

PLAN
MAIN·CORNICE

DROPS·UNDER·BRACKETS

DETAIL·AT·"A"

DOOR·PANEL·MOLD

JAMB
HEAD·SIMILAR

WINDOW·DETAIL

SILL.

SHINGLES.

PRESENT·GRADE.

SIDE·ELEVATION·

MEAS+DRAWN: KENNETH CLARK '29.

H O U S E ·

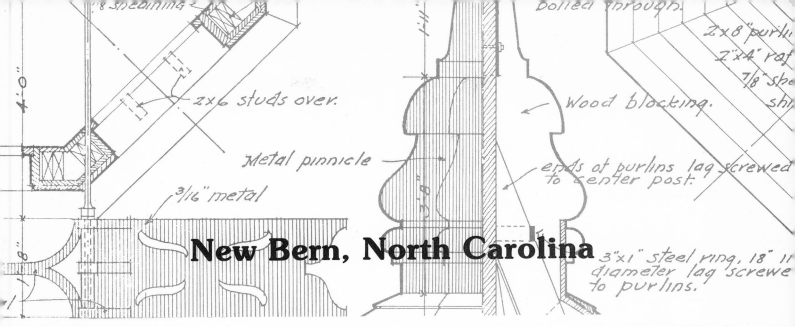

New Bern, North Carolina

I DOUBT whether the expert or the amateur alike, will find more and finer expressions of colonial architecture than are so happily presented in this ancient and well preserved seat of England's rule in North America. Here in New Bern, I dare say, the learned and artistic-minded Colonials were as charmed in their day, as we are now, with the sense of beauty nature has so lavishly distilled in eastern North Carolina. The superb trees and flowering shrubbery; the trumpeting loveliness of the landside; the broad, broad rivers; the semi-tropical climate; impelled them to have their houses stand unashamed in the midst of all this luxury.

Such environment and, maybe, too, the presence in New Bern of the "most beautiful residence in the Americas," the Royal Governor Tryon's palace, challenged their sense of proportion and architectural harmony. Anyhow, you can come to our romantic New Bern and find that what is here imaged forth is but a pallid picture of what rests yet untold.

New Bern, which was once called "Chattawka," is situated on a tongue of land between the Neuse and Trent rivers. The land was purchased from the Indian King Taylor by De Graffenried about 1710, when he joined the Swiss colonists who had embarked in Holland, sailed to northeast England and then for Carolina by way of Virginia.

In 1713 the settlement was broken up by Tuscarora Indians, but by November 1723 we find New Bern made a township covering two hundred and fifty acres and soon after it became the capital of the colony. It was the second town in North Carolina, Bath having been laid out in 1705. In the second year of the reign of George II the colony was sold to the Crown and the proprietary rights ceased. The first Royal Governor assumed his functions in 1731.

The population of New Bern in April 1775 was about six hundred. In 1792 there were about four hundred houses, all of wood excepting the Palace, the Church, the Gaol and two dwelling houses which were brick. By 1798, there were about 2000 people in the town and ship building was carried on extensively. The ropes, iron work and timber were of home manufacture. The designers and craftsmen who found outlets for their talent in the shipyards seem to have worked also hand in hand with the Guilds who wrought in brick and wood to provide a domestic architecture of great interest and beauty.

The first "show-place" of the town, Tryon's Palace, built in 1767, was designed by John Hawks, an architect who came to New Bern from the island of Malta. This three storied brick house with two storied wings, separated from the main building by curved colonnades, had a frontage of 87'-0" and a depth of 59'-0". £15,000 were raised by the people to pay the costs. Unfortunately it was burned in 1798 and only one wing is now standing. The absence of the "Palace," however, need not discourage the student and lover of early American architecture, for on almost every street one stands gratified in the presence of buildings which display real design and stunning craftsmanship.

The Groenendyke House, now known as the Hargett House, is a warm expression of ideals of comfort which the ancient merchants brought from Holland to our Carolina. One should not be surprised at the degree of preservation of these timbered homes. There were giant trees in those days; and only the eternal heart of them went into the making of colonial homes. Time was given to building them and no nails were used, where nails would disintegrate the fabric. Cozenly, an English Walnut tree stands by the Groenendyke House and, at front, two crimson laurels, their trunks fluted and spiral; and a rose tree, growing there, it would seem, when the arch-mason of the Carpenters' Guild spent loving days of labor on this so nobly simple house. I think you will want to repeat the comfort and spaciousness of this apparently small house. The fire-

HOUSE ON BROAD STREET, NEW BERN, NORTH CAROLINA

HOUSE AT 167 MIDDLE STREET, NEW BERN, NORTH CAROLINA

THE HANNAH CLARK HOUSE, CRAVEN STREET, NEW BERN, NORTH CAROLINA

place, you will surely want to repeat—I wonder whether we have added much to the things that really ease our weariness. Have we not abandoned the play of repose? I think great thoughts and tender fancies found food in the minds that clustered around the fireside in all our colonies. Well, anyway, our immortal men were to this manner born and reared. There was he who came out of Mt. Vernon; the Sage of Monticello;

much of his life in the gelid north but he has not found any scenes that this New Bern landside were ashamed to meet.

The "Louisiana" House, pictured below, stands facing the Neuse, and looking on to the south. Many a soulful watcher, I dare say, stood in the shade of that old gallery, looking for the homecoming of a sea-faring father, or a shining-eyed and weather-beaten lover.

THE "LOUISIANA" HOUSE, EAST FRONT STREET, NEW BERN, NORTH CAROLINA

the great wood-chopper and his log cabin; Andrew Jackson's shack here in Carolina; Alexander Hamilton. Thanks be! for the gathering love of ancient noble things.

There's little to choose between the climate of Louisiana and the coastal plain of North Carolina. So close are we to the fireside of the great Gulf Stream, that we do not shiver much here in winter; and in summer the breezes that come from the Neuse and the Trent, nights, sing "Always" to us. Fancy? Very well; take it so, if you will; but come and see. This writer lived

You should see the River Neuse, as it comes up almost to the feet of the "Louisiana" House. It is quite a mile and a half wide at this point; and as it moves on to the Sound, it widens and widens and widens. I seem to see it, a beautiful aisle, colonnaded by mossy water-oaks, umbrella pines and mimosa trees.

What influences one in the "Louisiana" House are spaciousness and tonal effects. I just don't know how to tell these things technically; but I feel them and enjoy them thoroughly.

The Presbyterian Church is a noble building. The patrician portico is eloquent. Plato, likely, dictated his immortal sentences near columns such as these. The building is fifty-five feet in width and seventy feet in length with a steeple rising to a height of one hundred and twenty-five feet. Three doors open into an ample vestibule whence two open into the audience room. The pulpit is between the two doors at the entrance into the audience chamber. The floor gradually ascends toward the rear of the church elevating the pews to give a clear vision of the pulpit.

It is little wonder that we find the Jarvis (Slover) House and the Smallwood House, following so soon after the completion of this jewel of an early American Church. To architects, these houses must be luscious bits; to us laymen, beautiful works and gardens of repose. I think they are doing mighty much to tell our people that the builders of this Republic were not only political scientists; but men of poetic feeling and artistic expression. If I dared, I should almost say that they vied with their architects in fidelity to harmony and composition. The exquisite detail of these houses gives us to think that what they sought was not curtailment of cost, but rather the fulfillment of an ideal.

THE MASONIC OPERA HOUSE
New Bern, North Carolina

Why those large and sculptured firesides? James Boyd, in "Drums," has a beautiful page that answers this question. Forensic art was developed there; classic lore had its chair there; political science was taught there.

When President George Washington came to New Bern in 1792, the Masonic Opera House was facing the Common, just as it is today. I do not know that I am reverent enough in speaking of this gracious old building, as quaint. I don't know that it represents any period; I do know it to be associated with the nobler sentiments of this community. One of its charms is the dignified lodge room on the upper floor.

A very "Kentucky Cardinal" of a Catholic priest lived in New Bern a hundred years ago. He had a very small congregation and was devoted to them. His love for his fellowman went out to the trees and song birds and his Irish terrier. It was such a person as this who built the little ridge-roofed house, with the delicate porch.

The Hannah Clark House has distinction and articulation. Houses of this character are passed a hundred times unnoticed. Then they are discovered!

George III, the George who forced our Declaration of Independence, was represented here by an able, kindly and courteous governor—William Tryon. New Bern was the seat of government in Carolina. Governor Tryon built, what in 1768, was regarded as the most pretentious house in America. George Street began at the entrance of the Tryon Palace; went north—the King's Highway—to Kingston; and then on to the summer capital, Hillsboro, the farthest point north of the colony. Naturally, along this street worthy homes were built. One of these is the Hanff House.

Of a piece with the Hanff House, is the Blackwell House, now owned by G. C. Eubanks. This charming residence was built by Josiah Blackwell, in 1774. Josiah Blackwell was a lumber merchant, and into this construction, went materials of a beautiful texture.

The doorway of the Nixon House, is like a "Mammy Crochet" Rose—colorful and daintily reminiscent of the days of long ago; a fitting portal to a gracious interior. This house on Craven Street is the only remaining example, in this section of New Bern, of the elegant town house of the early 19th century period.

Athens was cultured, indeed; and made of her language a most fluid and beautiful speech; but she is known best for her Parthenon and her undying Acropolis.

THE HANFF HOUSE, GEORGE STREET, NEW BERN, NORTH CAROLINA

A GAMBREL ROOF HOUSE, NEW BERN, NORTH CAROLINA

HOUSE ON HANCOCK STREET, NEW BERN, NORTH CAROLINA

THE BLACKWELL (TAYLOR) HOUSE, BROAD STREET, NEW BERN, NORTH CAROLINA

The MASONIC LODGE ROOM
NEW BERN, NORTH CAROLINA

WEST WALL OF THE MASONIC LODGE ROOM

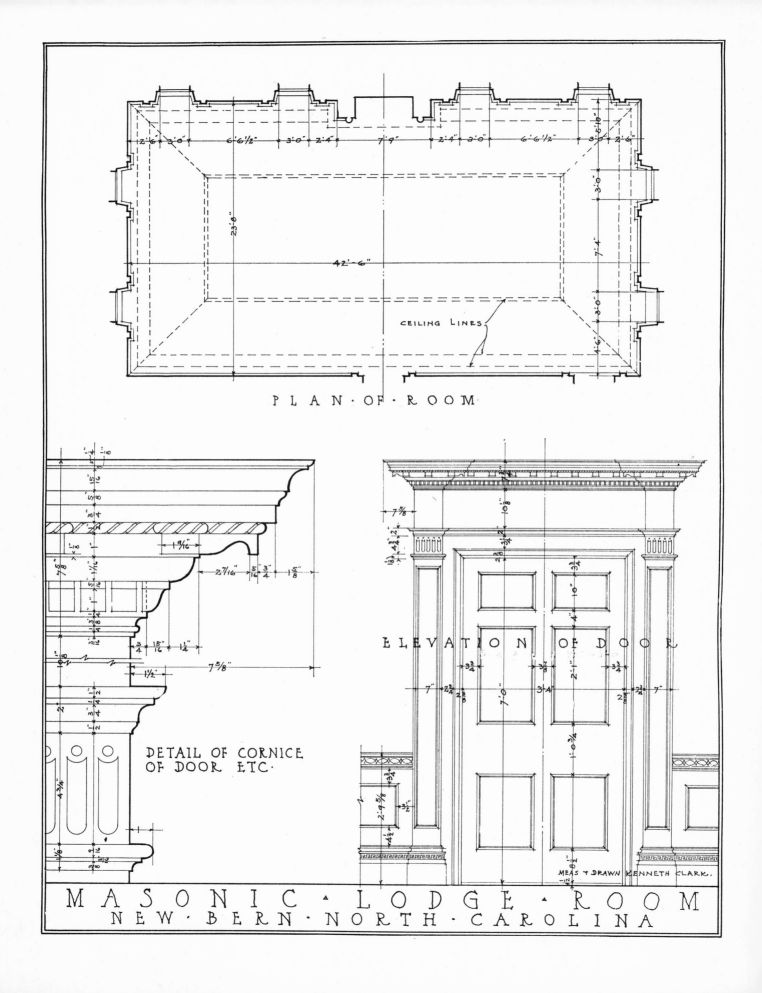

PLAN · OF · ROOM

CEILING LINES

DETAIL OF CORNICE
OF DOOR ETC·

ELEVATION OF DOOR

MEAS + DRAWN KENNETH CLARK·

MASONIC · LODGE · ROOM
NEW · BERN · NORTH · CAROLINA

DETAIL OF DOOR, MASONIC LODGE ROOM, NEW BERN, NORTH CAROLINA

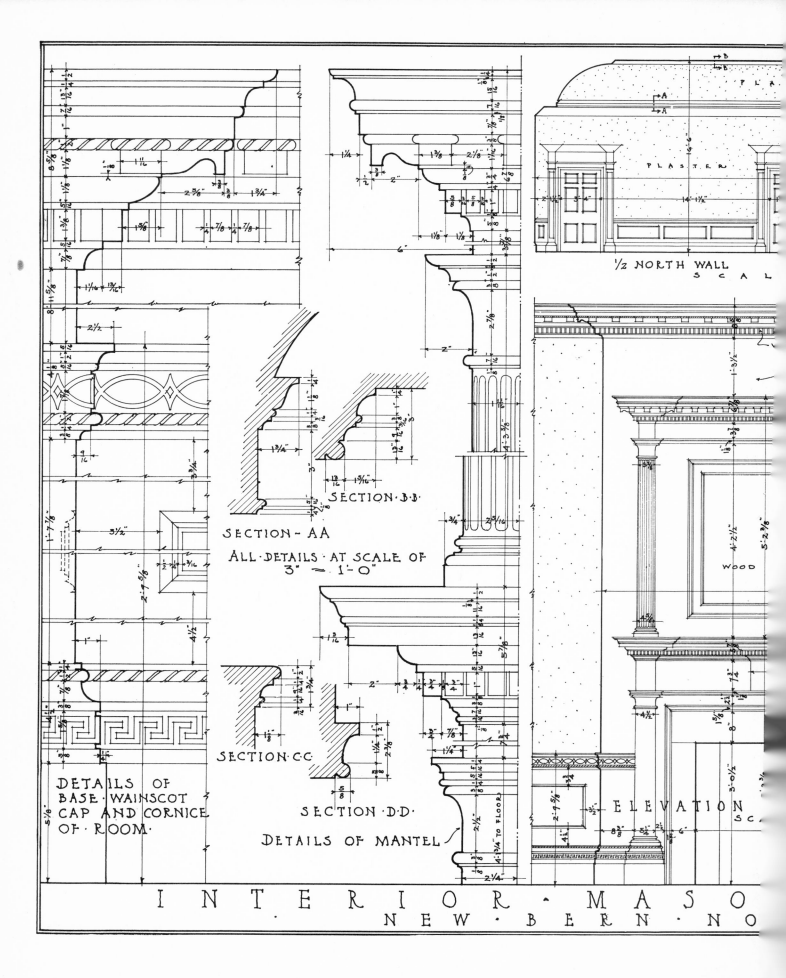

SECTION-B·B·

SECTION - AA

ALL·DETAILS·AT·SCALE·OF
3" = 1'-0"

SECTION·C·C·

DETAILS OF
BASE·WAINSCOT
CAP AND CORNICE
OF·ROOM·

SECTION ·D·D·

DETAILS OF MANTEL

½ NORTH WALL
SCAL

PLASTER

PLA

WOOD

ELEVATION
SC.

INTERIOR·MASO
NEW·BERN·NO

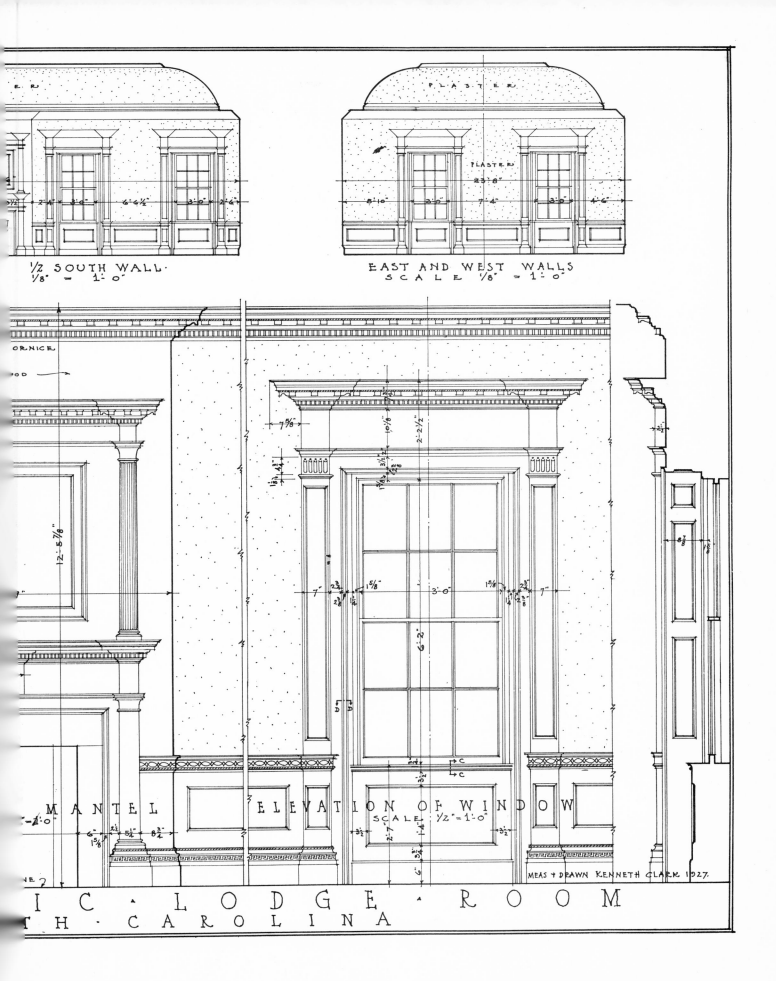

½ SOUTH WALL·
⅛" = 1'-0"

EAST AND WEST WALLS
S C A L E ⅛" = 1'-0"

PLASTER

PLASTER
23'-8"

2'-4" 3'-0" 6'-4½" 3'-2" 2'-4"

8'-10" 2'-0" 7'-4" 3'-0" 4'-6"

CORNICE

12'-5⅞"

7⅝

6'-2"

M A N T E L   E L E V A T I O N   O F   W I N D O W
SCALE ½"=1'-0"

MEAS + DRAWN KENNETH CLARK 1927.

I C · L O D G E · R O O M
T H · C A R O L I N A

THE HUGHES HOUSE, CRAVEN STREET, NEW BERN, NORTH CAROLINA
Torn down in 1925 and replaced by a garage!

THE NIXON HOUSE, CRAVEN STREET, NEW BERN, NORTH CAROLINA

Original steps removed when street was widened

The New England Influence in North Carolina

T HE antiquary of early American architecture will usually find himself able by mere inspection of an old house or even of a photograph of one to tell with reasonable accuracy in which of the provinces it is built; and if his acquaintance with the old work is slightly more than casual, to give the date of its construction within five or ten years. Once in a while, however, he runs across a building or group of buildings which is exceedingly puzzling; if he knows the locality in which they occur, he cannot understand how they happened to be there; and he will in some cases be able to say of the time of construction only "they *ought* to date from about 17–to 17–, but I can't say in this case exactly when they were built."

These cases are the most fascinating in the study of our early architecture; just as with the collector it is the odd piece, the freak, that commands the highest price, so in architecture it is the unusual and unexpected that arrest the attention. The piece of design, no matter how fine, that is just the solution that one might have expected of that especial problem in its particular locality at the exact date it was built, may be greatly admired for its architectural qualities, but does not arouse curiosity as does the building which makes one wonder how? and why? There are found, for example, houses of genuine Colonial design in southern Ohio, and yet everybody knows that Ohio was not settled until long after the Revolution and that a Colonial house is as little to be expected there as a Jacobean one. In Elizabeth City there still exist, or did some years ago, the decaying remnants of the oldest bank in North Carolina, a stucco, tiled roof building, which shows strong Spanish or Provencal influence; one wonders if it was designed by some emigrant from New Orleans, or if it was erected in conformity with the memories of some Huguenot refugee from southern France.

Such another town is New Bern. One would expect to find its architecture a sort of provincial copy of the great metropolis of Williamsburg, Virginia on the north, or (as Wilmington, N. C. indeed is) strongly flavored by the heavy beautiful Georgian of Charlestown; with the probability in favor of kinship with the Virginian type of Colonial, since North Carolina was settled rather through Norfolk than through Charlestown, and from the colonial period until today "the Carolinas" are much less allied to each other than North Carolina is with Virginia or South Carolina with Georgia. Actually we find its resemblance to either very slight indeed; but strangely enough, its lovely and elaborate houses, dating from the opening years of the nineteenth century would have passed without remark anywhere in New England of the late eighteenth, and they especially resemble the Salem of Samuel MacIntyre.

The causes of the resemblance (and these must have been compelling causes) are difficult or impossible to discover. In the similar case of the little hamlet of Clinton in southeastern Georgia, the local tradition provides a satisfactory solution. Clinton has only three or four houses of any size, all very much alike, and of a workmanship far superior to the average slovenly craftsmanship of the negro slaves who furnished the mechanics in the country districts of the south before the war. The detail is much less in scale than that in any of the surrounding districts, is far more elaborate, better designed, and distinctly earlier in feeling than the period at which it was built. Inquiry revealed that Clinton was settled about 1815 by emigrants from the northern part of Vermont, in which the Colonial tradition had not yet been superseded by that of the Greek revival, and where the intelligent and thorough craftsmanship of the colonial cabinet maker still persisted. This hamlet became a sort of center for fine furniture; the few families from Vermont became wealthy from the products of their skill, and built for themselves houses as fine in design and probably larger than those they had left behind in Vermont; a few surviving chairs and

THE JUDGE DONALD HOUSE, 163 CRAVEN STREET, NEW BERN, NORTH CAROLINA

ENTRANCE DETAIL—THE JUDGE DONALD HOUSE, NEW BERN, NORTH CAROLINA

tables of austere and delicate line, of maple or mahogany or walnut, scattered about Eastern Georgia reinforce the tradition.

No such definite evidence is available in the case of New Bern. On the contrary there are several confused, conflicting and indefinite traditions as to the designers of the old houses, and even with a good deal of research exact dates cannot be assigned to the buildings themselves. The customary statement is of course that they were all pre-Revolutionary; and that they were designed by Sir Christopher Wren or one of his pupils. Sir Chris-

out into civil work. This is plausible, but as the work bears no close resemblance to English Georgian and is very similar indeed to the late New England Colonial, the internal evidence would seem sufficient to give a negative answer to this tradition of derivation. It is of course possible that an English naval architect of some constructive skill and architectural imagination, called upon, in the absence of any more regularly trained architect, to design houses for his friends, would buy some books of design of American authorship and, following them as closely as he could, achieve approxi-

THE JOHN WRIGHT STANLY HOUSE, NEW BERN, NORTH CAROLINA

topher Wren's pupils and George Washington's pew are the inevitable pleasant and ridiculous traditions current in all old towns and about all old churches; the mere fact that a church was built in 1810, while Wren died in 1723 and Washington in 1799, does not prevent the prideful custodian from pointing out the spire designed by Wren, and the pew occupied by Washington. The Washington tradition is feeble in New Bern but the Wren tradition is strong.

Another legend is that much of the later work was designed by an English architect, James Coor, who came to New Bern as a naval architect and branched

mately such houses as we find in New Bern. This is a sufficiently reasonable explanation, but based on a good many assumptions, any of which may be false; and if any one is false, the whole theory falls to the ground.

Another tradition is that the ships of New Bern departed on their voyages up the coast laden with leaf tobacco and molasses for the Salem factories to transform into smoking tobacco and rum for the pious New Englanders, and returned with furniture and wood-work, doors, mantels, and wainscot from the Salem makers. This again seems a perfectly tenable hypothesis, until we discover that the material of which the cabinet work

LAW OFFICE ADJOINING THE WASHINGTON BRYAN HOUSE, NEW BERN, NORTH CAROLINA

of New Bern is composed is not the northern white pine so beloved by the New England craftsman, but the native long leaf pine of North Carolina, and unless we assume that the ships which carried north the tobacco and molasses, carried long leaf pine timber to be worked up in New England, this pretty theory goes by the board. It is known that New Bern was in these early days and for many years thereafter a port from which much lumber was exported, and this may have happened; New England was already fairly well settled along the seaboard, and a lumber shortage was beginning to be felt; but even with due allowance for these

merce of New Bern was largely with New England, and with Salem and Boston in particular, the New England architecture was seen, admired, and imitated. Certainly the designs are copied from the same handbooks used in New England, instead of the English books used further to the south; and New England mechanics may have acted as foremen and instructors. That is the case in many parts of the south today, and very likely was a hundred years ago.

Whatever its genesis, we can be grateful for the results obtained in this, the most prolific in good architecture of all the little cities of the south. The town for-

THE JUDGE DONALD HOUSE—163 CRAVEN STREET, NEW BERN, NORTH CAROLINA
(From an old photograph by Wooten - Moulton Studio)

things, it seems entirely improbable that New England mechanics would have used the hard brittle yellow pine for the complicated carvings so common in New Bern, when they could have and did procure for all their other work the soft, even-grained white pine.

One guess as to the origin of this lovely architecture is as good as another,—'you pays your money and you takes your choice'; mine is that when the town began to grow rapidly, as it did just after the Revolution, it did what all other little cities did; used its local talent for design and construction, and the local talent used the books they could find most easily. Since the com-

tunately escaped the vicissitudes of the Civil war, and preserved most of its old buildings intact; and since the population and wealth have grown very slowly during the last hundred years, it has also escaped that far more deadly enemy of fine old architecture, progress. Where are our old houses in New York and Philadelphia, or Boston? Those that still survive are museums or the homes of societies; but in New Bern they are still part of the daily life of the community; not thrust forward for admiration with "Do not touch" signs, on every corner, but used as they were intended to be, warm with human life and illumined with hospitality.

LAW OFFICE ADJOINING THE JUDGE DONALD HOUSE, NEW BERN, NORTH CAROLINA

SECOND FLOOR DRAWING ROOM
THE SMALLWOOD HOUSE
NEW BERN, NORTH CAROLINA

MANTEL—NORTH WALL OF DRAWING ROOM

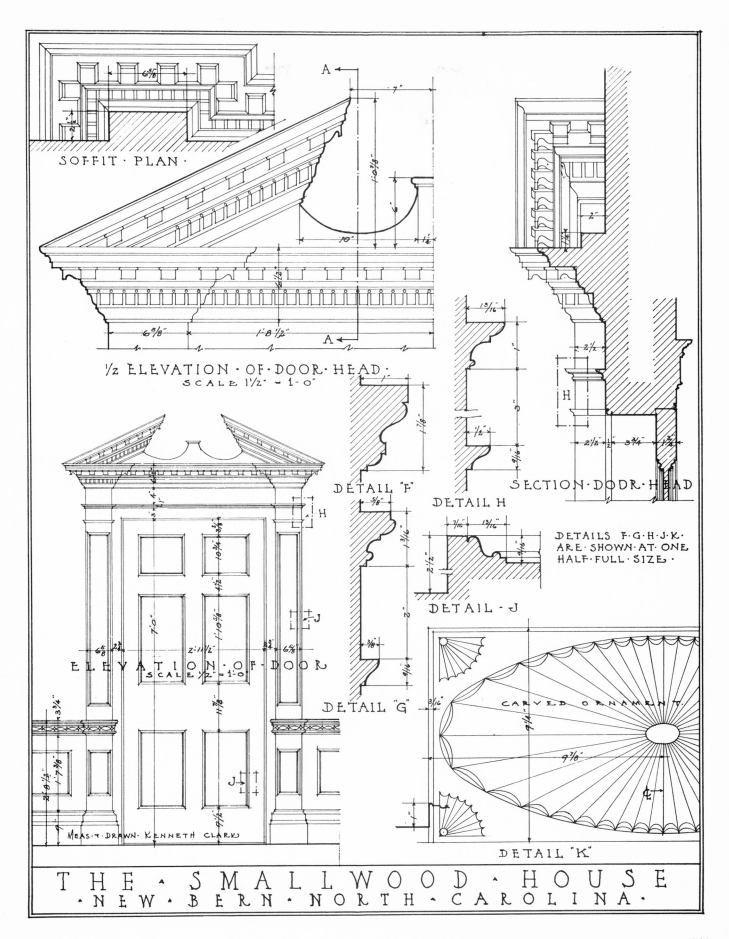

SOFFIT · PLAN ·

½ ELEVATION · OF · DOOR · HEAD ·
SCALE 1½" = 1-0"

DETAIL "F"

DETAIL H

SECTION · DOOR · HEAD

DETAILS F·G·H·J·K·
ARE · SHOWN · AT · ONE
HALF · FULL · SIZE ·

DETAIL · J

ELEVATION · OF · DOOR
SCALE ½" = 1-0

DETAIL "G"

CARVED ORNAMENT

DETAIL "K"

MEAS. & DRAWN · KENNETH CLARK

THE · SMALLWOOD · HOUSE
· NEW · BERN · NORTH · CAROLINA ·

141

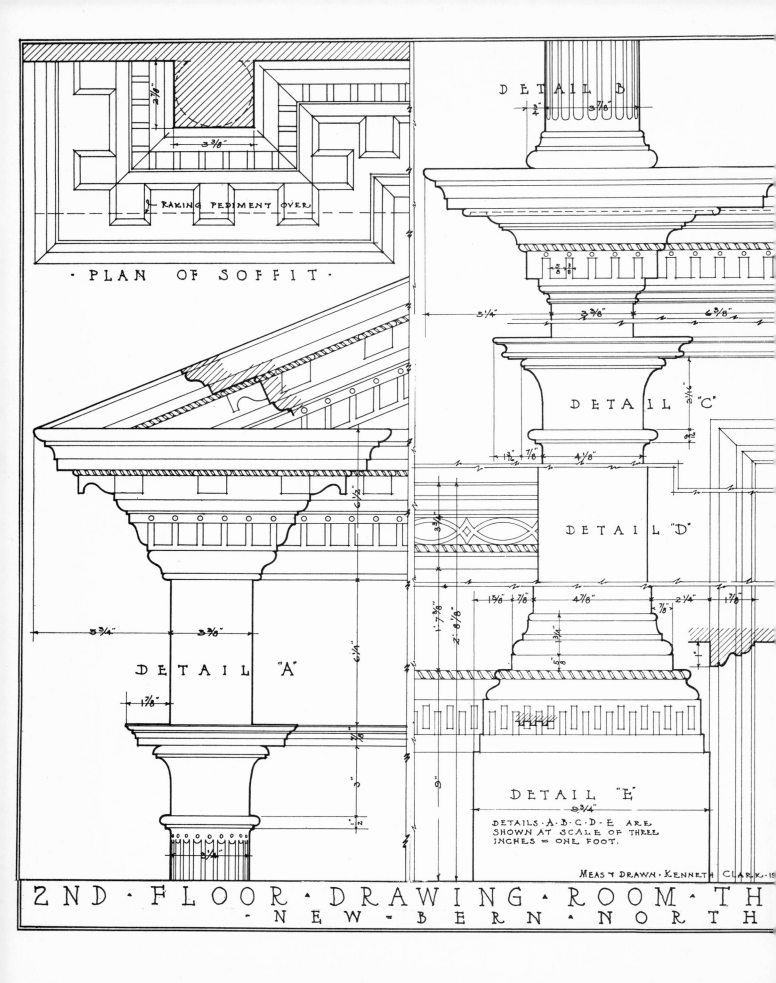

· PLAN · OF · SOFFIT ·

RAKING PEDIMENT OVER

DETAIL B

DETAIL "C"

DETAIL "D"

DETAIL "A"

DETAIL "E"

DETAILS · A · B · C · D · E · ARE
SHOWN AT SCALE OF THREE
INCHES = ONE FOOT.

MEAS't DRAWN · KENNETH CLARK · 19

2ND · FLOOR · DRAWING · ROOM · TH
· NEW · BERN · NORTH

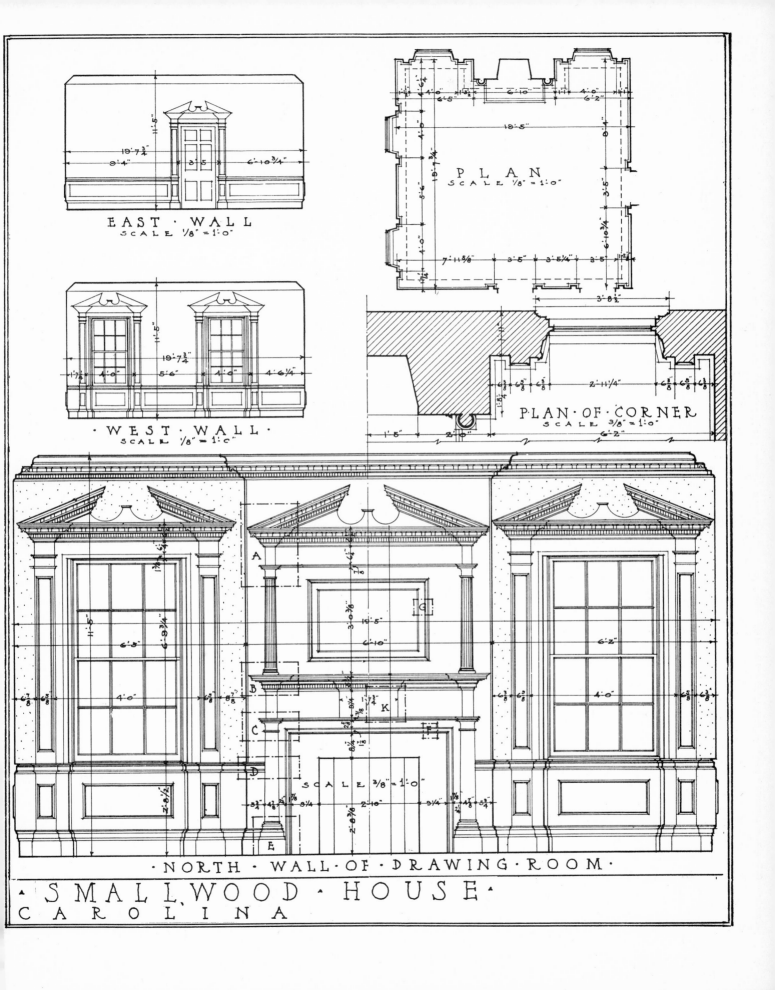

EAST · WALL
SCALE ⅛" = 1'·0"

P L A N
SCALE ⅛" = 1'·0"

· WEST · WALL ·
SCALE ⅛" = 1'·0"

PLAN · OF · CORNER
SCALE ⅜" = 1'·0"

· NORTH · WALL · OF · DRAWING · ROOM ·

· S M A L L W O O D · H O U S E ·
C A R O L I N A

THE SMALLWOOD HOUSE, NEW BERN, NORTH CAROLINA

THE STEVENSON HOUSE, POLLOCK STREET   HOUSE ON CRAVEN STREET

TYPICAL HOUSES WITH "CAPTAIN'S WALK" AND ORNAMENTAL RAILING — NEW BERN, NORTH CAROLINA

THE ROBERTS HOUSE, NEW BERN, NORTH CAROLINA

HOUSE ON THE C. D. BRADHAM PROPERTY, NEW BERN, NORTH CAROLINA

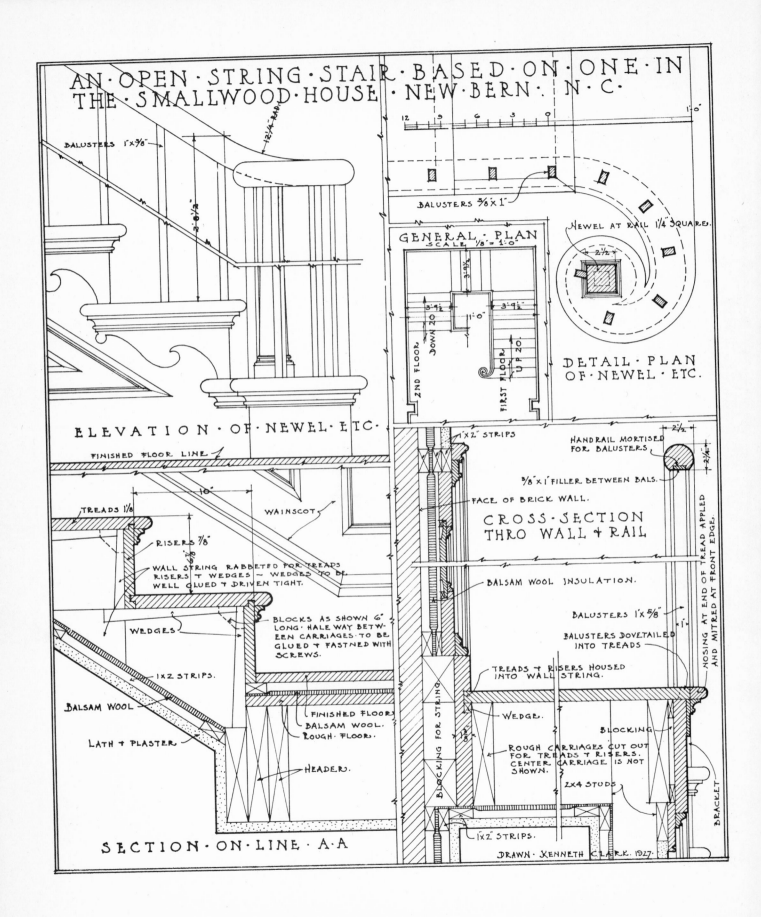

AN·OPEN·STRING·STAIR·BASED·ON·ONE·IN
THE·SMALLWOOD·HOUSE·NEW·BERN·N·C·

BALUSTERS 1"x⅞"

12¼ RAD.

3'-6½"

BALUSTERS ⅝"x 1"

GENERAL·PLAN
SCALE ⅛" = 1'-0"

2ND·FLOOR
DOWN 20

3'-9½"
1'-0"

3'-9½"

FIRST·FLOOR
UP 20

NEWEL AT RAIL 1¼ SQUARE.

2½

DETAIL·PLAN
OF·NEWEL·ETC.

ELEVATION·OF·NEWEL·ETC·

FINISHED·FLOOR·LINE

10"

WAINSCOT

TREADS 1⅛

RISERS ⅞"

6⅞

WALL STRING RABBETED FOR TREADS
RISERS ↑ WEDGES — WEDGES TO BE
WELL GLUED ↑ DRIVEN TIGHT.

WEDGES

1x2 STRIPS.

BALSAM WOOL

LATH ↑ PLASTER

BLOCKS AS SHOWN 6"
LONG · HALF WAY BETW-
EEN CARRIAGES·TO·BE
GLUED ↑ FASTNED WITH
SCREWS.

FINISHED FLOOR.
BALSAM WOOL.
ROUGH·FLOOR.

HEADER.

SECTION·ON·LINE·A A

1"x 2" STRIPS

HANDRAIL MORTISED
FOR BALUSTERS

2½

2¼

⅝"x1" FILLER BETWEEN BALS.

FACE OF BRICK WALL.

CROSS·SECTION
THRO WALL ↑ RAIL

BALSAM WOOL INSULATION.

BALUSTERS 1"x ⅝"

BALUSTERS DOVETAILED
INTO TREADS

TREADS ↑ RISERS HOUSED
INTO WALL STRING.

WEDGE.

BLOCKING

ROUGH CARRIAGES CUT OUT
FOR TREADS ↑ RISERS.
CENTER CARRIAGE IS NOT
SHOWN.

2x4 STUDS

1"x2" STRIPS.

BLOCKING FOR STRING

1⅛

NOSING AT END OF TREAD APPLED
AND MITRED AT FRONT EDGE.

BRACKET

DRAWN KENNETH CLARK 1927.

150

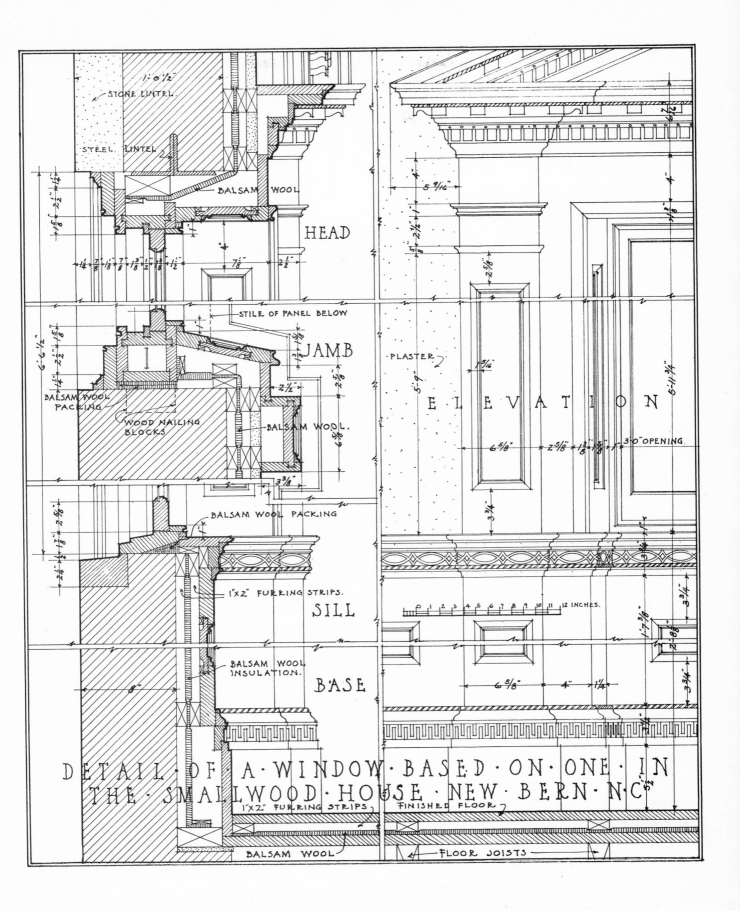

DETAIL · OF · A · WINDOW · BASED · ON · ONE · IN
THE · SMALLWOOD · HOUSE · NEW · BERN · N·C·

STONE LINTEL

STEEL LINTEL

BALSAM WOOL

HEAD

STILE OF PANEL BELOW

JAMB

BALSAM WOOL PACKING

WOOD NAILING BLOCKS

BALSAM WOOL

BALSAM WOOL PACKING

1"x2" FURRING STRIPS.

SILL

BALSAM WOOL INSULATION.

BASE

1"x2" FURRING STRIPS

BALSAM WOOL

PLASTER

ELEVATION

3·0" OPENING

12 INCHES.

FINISHED FLOOR

FLOOR JOISTS

151

Group of Old Houses from St. Philip's Churchyard

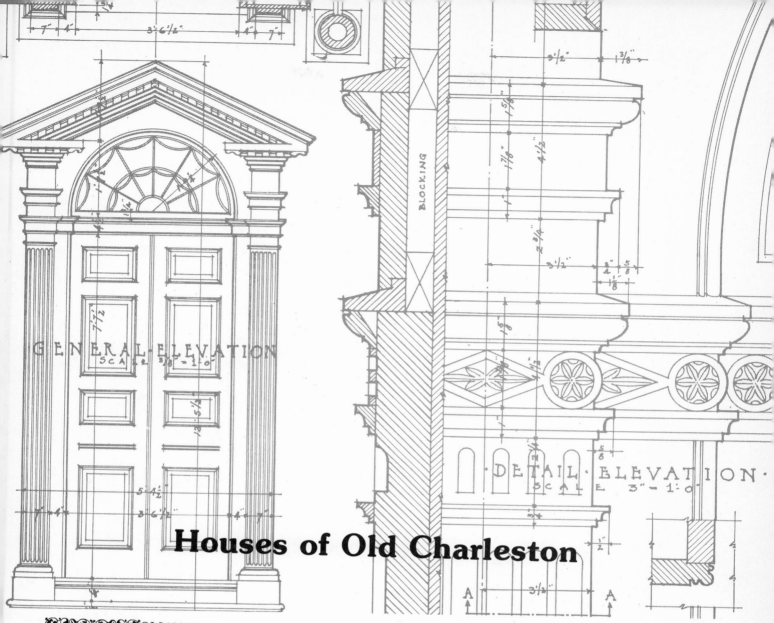

GENERAL·ELEVATION·
SCALE 3/8=1'-0"

·DETAIL·ELEVATION·
SCALE 3"=1'-0"

BLOCKING

Houses of Old Charleston

ROMANCE, COLOR and an ATMOSPHERE of the old world are depicted most vividly in sub-tropical Charleston. The student of architecture and the artist, alike, may experience the refreshment and tonic of a trip abroad as they poke about this beguiling old sea-port and "summer resort" of Colonial America.

Fascinating vistas and compositions that are ever varied and delightful are seen throughout the city as one strolls up and down the narrow, mellow, old streets.

The Cavalier and the Hugenot left behind them a quaint mixture of English and French ideas of building and adornment, to which were added the influences of the San Dominican and West Indian settlers and the emigrants from the Low Countries of Europe. Their building is thoroughly adapted to the demands of the climate and the hospitable life of the Southern planter. The typical house is built on a line with the sidewalk, the narrow end and porch entrance on the street and

enormous two or three story verandas facing on a side garden. High walls of brick and wood hide the gardens from the passer-by, but glimpses may be seen through the lacy patterns of the hand wrought iron gates.

The materials of construction are foreign in character. Brick, wood, Bermuda stone and oyster shell lime stucco in different colors, give a varied ensemble that is not at all consistent with the general idea of our early settlements. Salmon pink and purple black, moss spotted tile roofs add a subtle touch of color, as do the thick variegated slates and ancient shingles. The strange variety of roof intersections, unsymmetrical elevations, jutting wrought iron balconies and the way the buildings are placed in relation to the streets, make us feel that Charleston is the most "foreign" city in the United States.

Charleston justly claims an ancient and royal pedigree which through all the viscissitudes of two and a half centuries has left its stamp deeply imprinted. The ravages of two wars, in both of which this city played a

On Calhoun Street looking toward Second Presbyterian Church

St. Michael's East looking toward Meeting Street

Gates—Izard-Edwards-Smyth House, 14 *Legaré Street*

Spire of St. Philip's Church from
Graveyard of the Huguenot Church

conspicuous part, numerous general conflagrations and the earthquake of 1886 have caused the loss of many of her beautiful buildings. There is preserved, however, a wealth of uniquely interesting architecture.

It has seemed to us that the buildings cannot be studied properly apart from their surroundings. To look comprehendingly up at church spires and splendid town houses, one must also look beyond them at the city and the people and the times that created them. To appreciate old Charleston at its fullest value it is necessary to see, not only the architectural monuments, but also their settings, and to catch the spirit and atmosphere of the place. It is for these reasons that we have selected the accompanying photographs as illustrations for this introduction to Charleston. They will be a revelation to those who do not know the old town and an awakening of pleasant memories to those who do.

In the absence of any natural altitudes, the city lying on a peninsula as flat as a board between the two rivers, Ashley on the west and Cooper on the east, it is difficult to obtain a comprehensive view of the whole place. There are, however, many viewpoints hidden behind buildings or in the church yards where it is impossible not to be moved by the lure of the surroundings. It does not require much imagination when walking through St. Michaels Alley or wandering in St. Philips grave-yard to believe that America is three thousand miles away.

The visitor cannot escape the charm of Old Charleston—a charm which can only be suggested by Kenneth Clark's photographs. They will serve to recall to mind the extent of the debt our new world architecture owes to its European ancestry. Nowhere else in America, except possibly New Orleans and Quebec, can one discover a background so haunted by memories of the old world.

*On Church Street,
looking toward First
Presbyterian Church*

Church Street approaching Tradd Street—Brewton—Sawter House

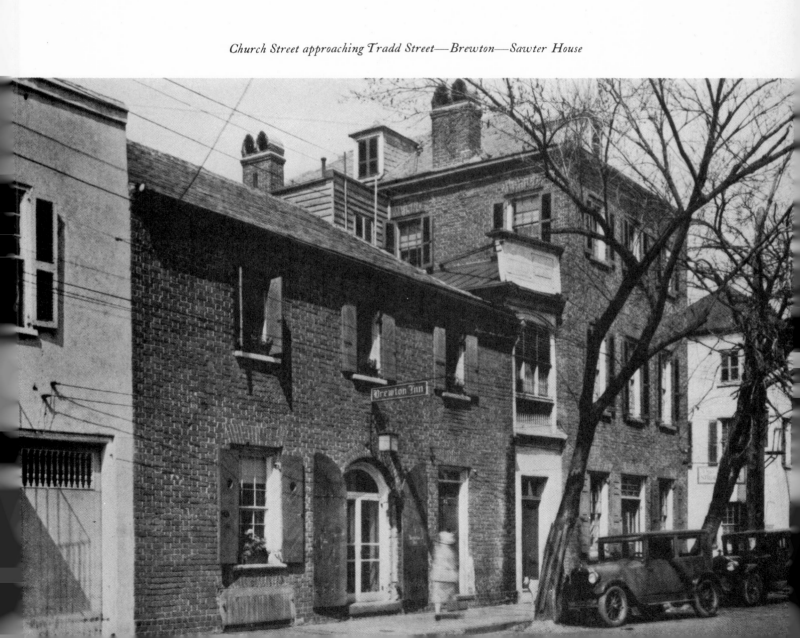

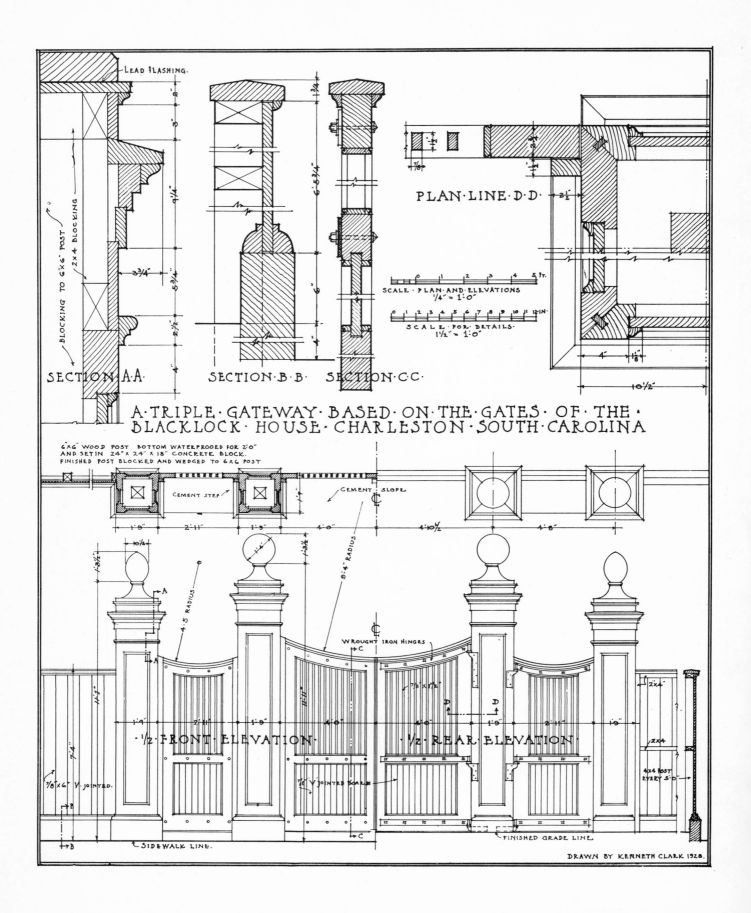

SECTION·A·A. SECTION·B·B. SECTION·C·C.

PLAN·LINE·D·D·

SCALE · PLAN · AND · ELEVATIONS
1/4" = 1'-0"

SCALE · FOR · DETAILS ·
1 1/2" = 1'-0"

A·TRIPLE·GATEWAY·BASED·ON·THE·GATES·OF·THE· BLACKLOCK·HOUSE·CHARLESTON·SOUTH·CAROLINA

6"x6" WOOD POST BOTTOM WATERPROOFED FOR 2'-0"
AND SET IN 24"x 24" x 18" CONCRETE BLOCK.
FINISHED POST BLOCKED AND WEDGED TO 6x6 POST

CEMENT STEP CEMENT SLOPE

WROUGHT IRON HINGES

·1/2·FRONT·ELEVATION·   ·1/2·REAR·ELEVATION·

7/8"x6" V·JOINTED.

1/6 V·JOINTED SCALE

SIDEWALK LINE.

FINISHED GRADE LINE

4x4 POST EVERY 5'-0"

DRAWN BY KENNETH CLARK 1928.

HOUSES AT 25 AND 27 MEETING STREET, CHARLESTON, SOUTH CAROLINA

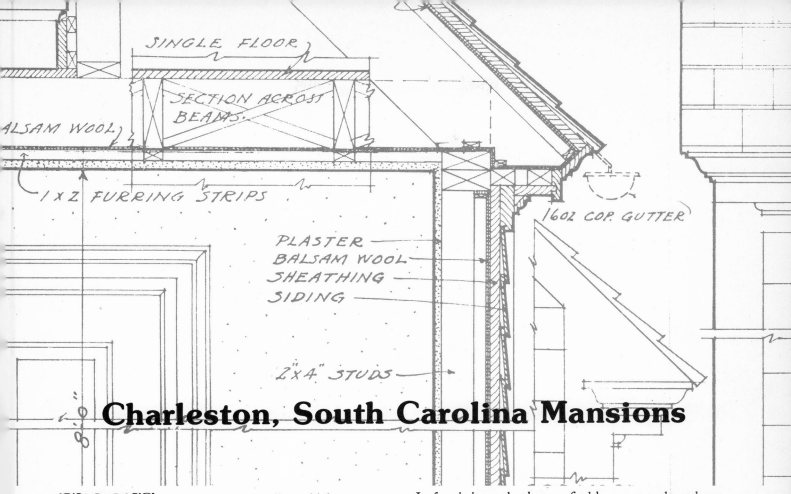

SINGLE FLOOR

SECTION ACROSS
BEAMS.

ALSAM WOOL

1 X 2 FURRING STRIPS

PLASTER
BALSAM WOOL
SHEATHING
SIDING

2"X4" STUDS

1602 COP. GUTTER

Charleston, South Carolina Mansions

IF THERE is one quality which more than any other seems to run like a beneficial alloy through all our Colonial architecture it is its distinct friendliness:—its human scale and hominess. One sees this most convincingly in the minimum house of the early followers of husbandry in New England, and as one proceeds further south through the Middle Atlantic States and the scale and elegance of the early habitations increase, there seems no diminution of this fortunate quality.

Still further south in the softer climes where easily obtainable labor made living more leisurely, and the scale of the house increases commensurately, one might expect greater severity of social intercourse; but always there seems to remain that atmosphere of hospitable companionship. In the city of Charleston, South Carolina, one pauses before one of the most grandiose of early Colonial residences in a not notably important street (except that it is named King Street) and finds its portico almost on the sidewalk line, but separated from it by iron gates and a spiked whorl above the fence which is so extreme in its violent convolutions as to remind one of the barking dog which has no bite, and to produce more a feeling of amusement than any other at the extreme battle array. So still the feeling is one of friendliness and it is probable that the placing of the mansion in close proximity to the street operates here, as in New England, to dispel any feeling of aloofness.

In fact it is rarely that we find large grounds and gardens in connection with any village or urban example of this subtle type of architecture,—even the examples in the country being placed as a usual thing inconspicuously. Only when we encounter the mansions of Philadelphia in Fairmount Park, and our two most notable examples of spacious surrounding grounds—Mt. Vernon, and Westover on the James River—do we find park-like proportions in the setting of the houses, and then nothing commensurate, say, with The Priory just out of Bath, England and many, many others there of Georgian type. In our two examples, the river is but a short distance from the house and the nearness in each case bespeaks ease of intercourse and friendliness.

The Miles Brewton Mansion is one of the few early houses which has survived several disastrous fires in the city, but it was antedated by a similar one built by Honorable Charles Pinckney.

Although placed so near the street line there is ample garden space in the rear. The large gate posts flanking the entrance to the stable court on one side of the house form an impressive feature which one finds constantly recurring throughout the city:—a comparatively small house frequently having this lordly feature. And several times one sees, as here, a glimpse of the stable playfully designed as "something different" with a primitive form reminiscent of Tudor England. Here is a glimpse of another feature which astounds northerners, the Spanish type of tiled roof, until one recalls the constant early

intercourse with the West Indies, close by, and realizes that the frequent fires of the city made imperative a fireproof roofing. Many examples of this type of roofing existed until recent years in Charleston and in the immediate past they have been still further depleted.

Most fittingly, however, is this type of roof still preserved on the Old Powder Magazine—originally a picturesque part of a Bastion of the City Wall and the only early building remaining in Charleston which of a surety was built in the Seventeenth Century.

The interior details of the Brewton-Sawter house here shown exhibit a rather curious divergence from the more usual type around Charleston;—something recalling mantels further north around New York, where the fanlike spandril form in the upper corners of the frieze was used quite commonly as well as the radiating lines of the oval in the center panel. The identical use of the wainscot cap throughout the lower part of the entablature of the mantel which is simplified by this substitution for the pilaster cap is not exactly unusual, but being attractively enriched calls special attention to the feature and seems to tie the mantel proper into the general finish of the room. This "entablature" of most mantels is so free in its departure from strictly classical proportions in its relation of cornice to exaggerated frieze and suppressed architrave,—in this instance like the wainscot cap,—that it hardly warrants the nomenclature, except that early English examples such as those of Gibbs and Milton—which abide by classic divisions more closely, have fixed the tradition. Other details of this room are hardly as happy, such as the great width and multiplicity of mouldings in the architraves surrounding the windows: the awkward way in which the cornice of the room begins by a plump ovolo suggesting that the true beginning of the cornice may have been covered by the plaster of the ceiling: the shapeless brackets and the profusion of mouldings immediately above the dentil course as well as immediately below it. Then too, there is the detrimental use of a frieze of striking ornament further made noticeable by the use of rosettes,—those circular whorls which easily become too prominent if of much size.

The custom in most of the Charleston houses of note of placing the main floor of the house over a basement entirely above ground offered a great opportunity for that distinction which invariably comes from well designed steps. Often the drawing room was on the second floor above the basement offering an opportunity for elongated proportions in the upper stories resulting in added dignity of effect. The Miles Brewton house has the first floor placed much lower than most of the notable houses as this custom seems to have been a gradual

growth perhaps resulting through frequent communication with the West Indies, causing the builders to gradually elevate the important stories. This feature together with the tiled roof, offers two points of departure from the usual Colonial architecture of the rest of the States and makes the work of this city and its surrounding towns and plantation houses distinct.

A simple rendering of this feature is shown in the two houses built by Daniel Blake in Court House Square with an arched entrance at the side walk level, making a common service entrance for both, while the main entrances are at a considerably higher level and reached by attractive steps and landing.

The admirable Bull-Blacklock House, 18 Bull Street, built in 1800 is a splendid example of the treatment of this feature while the impressiveness of the large carriage entrance gates and posts places the architectural

HOUSE AT 301 EAST BAY, SOUTH, CHARLESTON, SOUTH CAROLINA   *Built about* 1800

THE RALPH IZARD HOUSE, 110 BROAD STREET, CHARLESTON, SOUTH CAROLINA
Built before 1757

value of the house well up among the mansions of the town. Here again we see the use of wooden gates both for the carriage entrance and the more intimate service entrance of the house, the latter being enriched to a point which apparently shows a substitution of wood for iron either as a matter of economy or the inability to get iron work of the character which is indicative of the city.

The characteristic type of Charleston house belonging to this City alone, and finally arrived at through climatic requirements and manner of living, is seen in considerable statliness in the Henry Manigault House at 18 Meeting Street, is shown here. The long living room frontage is toward the garden and the narrow end of the house on the street, with entrance door in a prolongation of the first floor street facade, the door bell of which reaches distant regions in the service ell and invariably results in a long wait for the caller.

To the already great variety of types of houses in the architectural ensemble of this remarkable city,—influenced as it was by the direct English strain:—that of the French Hugenot influx in the latter part of the Seventeenth Century; with the slight touches of the doughty Dutch from Nova-Belgia and the quiescent Quaker, and still further by the Spanish influence from the West Indies,—there is added a strikingly northern note—even of New England—in the charming house built by one Nathaniel Russell (a name from the heart of New England) distinctly different from all the others except that it adapts one major and unique Charlestonian feature, and even here seen only semi-occasionally,—that of the many sided bay. In this case it is, if memory serves, a half elongated octagon on the exterior, its farthest projection being the point of an angle and becoming a circular room within by a padding of its interior angles. Of this remarkable feature there is another fine example still extant in the Middleton House and a legend exists of another one on the East Battery which was destroyed. This surprising and thoroughly delightful feature being treated in splendid scale in both the Russell and Middleton houses has a most satisfying charm. From the delicate balustrade of the roof down through the well proportioned cornice, the perfection of window lintels, and well proportioned key-blocked arches to the iron balconies of a detail common to New England in design, but here adopting a local variation in a beautiful shape which bows out in the center of each window on the street facade,—all is satisfaction. The form of the belt-course between the second and third stories seems the only divergence from the New England type, and the circular caps of iron bolts somewhat interrupting the belt course attest a comparatively recent addition of iron rods through the building necessitated by the unfortunate racking of earthquake tremors.

The fence alone is the sole disappointing feature in this beautiful and distinct piece of architecture, it apparently being either a comparatively recent substitution or may indicate a sudden disaster to Charleston architecture by the death or removal of the remarkable artisan who did such wonderful work in the way of embellishing the gates and balconies of this beautiful city.

THE NATHANIEL RUSSELL HOUSE,
51 MEETING STREET,
CHARLESTON, SOUTH CAROLINA
Built before 1811

THE WILLIAM
BLACKLOCK HOUSE,
18 BULL STREET,
CHARLESTON,
SOUTH CAROLINA

THE MILES BREWTON HOUSE,
27 KING STREET,
CHARLESTON, SOUTH CAROLINA

Iron Entrance Gate, Fence and Stable

167

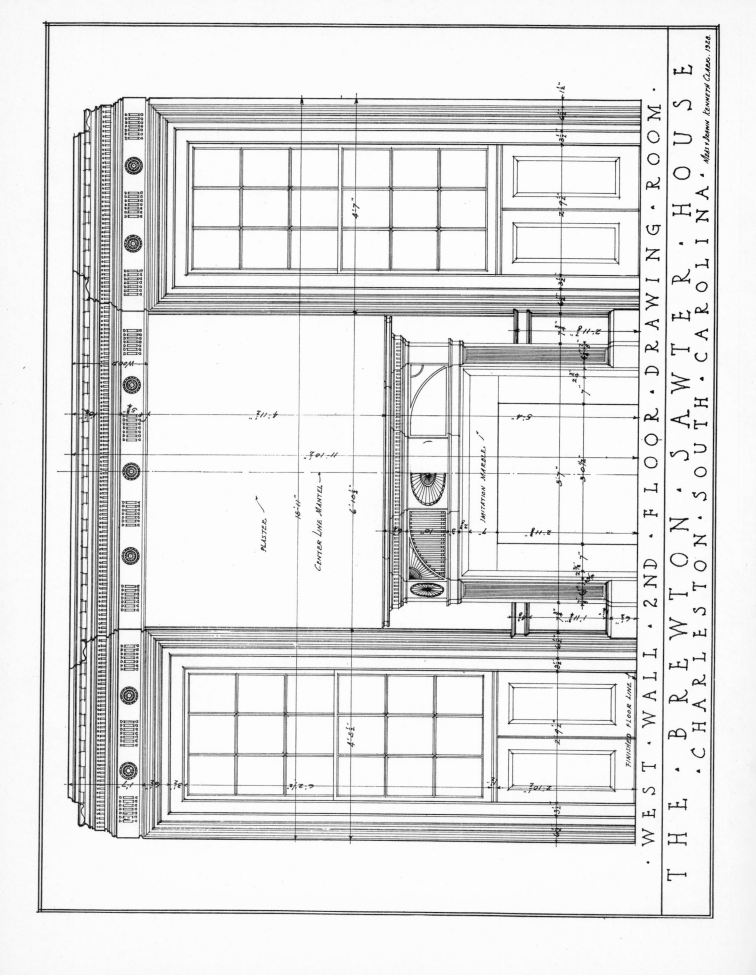

· WEST · WALL · 2ND · FLOOR · DRAWING · ROOM ·

· THE · BREWTON · SAWTER · HOUSE ·

· CHARLESTON · SOUTH · CAROLINA ·

Meas. + Drawn. Kenneth Clark. 1928.

THE BREWTON-SAWTER HOUSE
CORNER OF CHURCH AND TRADD STREETS
CHARLESTON, SOUTH CAROLINA

MEASURED DRAWINGS *from*
The George F. Lindsay Collection

West Wall—Second Floor Drawing Room

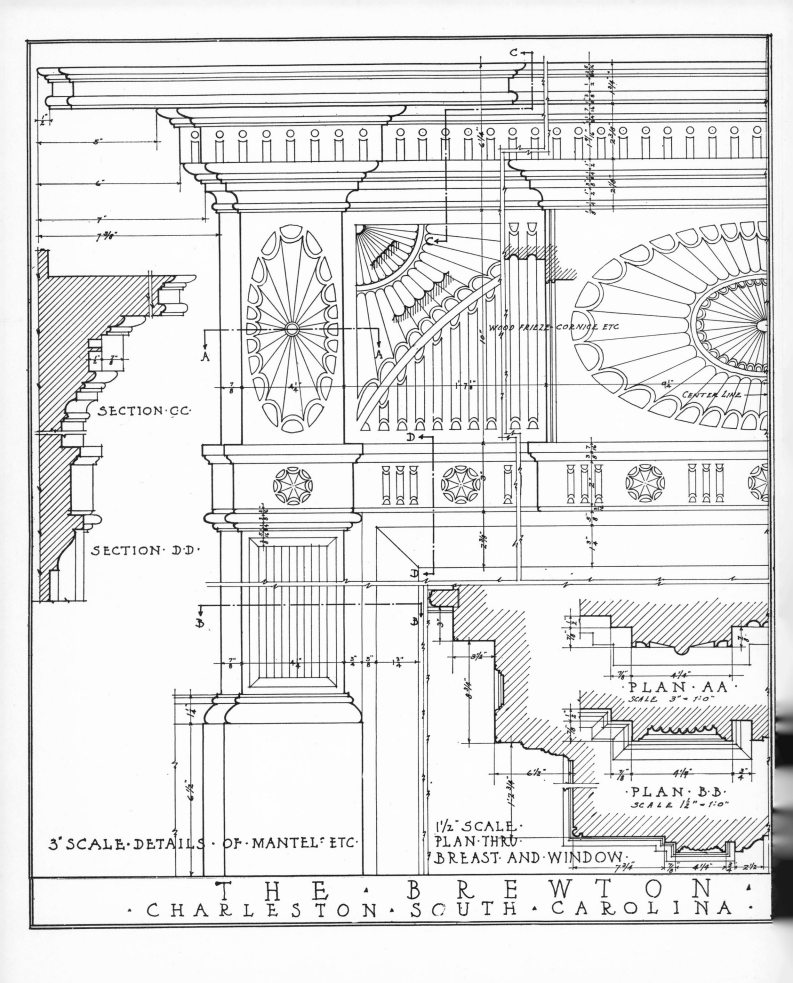

SECTION·CC·

SECTION·D·D·

WOOD·FRIEZE·CORNICE·ETC·

CENTER LINE

PLAN·AA·
SCALE 3" = 1'·0"

PLAN·B·B·
SCALE 1½" = 1'·0"

3"·SCALE·DETAILS·OF·MANTEL·ETC·

·1½"·SCALE·
PLAN·THRU·
BREAST·AND·WINDOW·

·THE·BREWTON·
·CHARLESTON·SOUTH·CAROLINA·

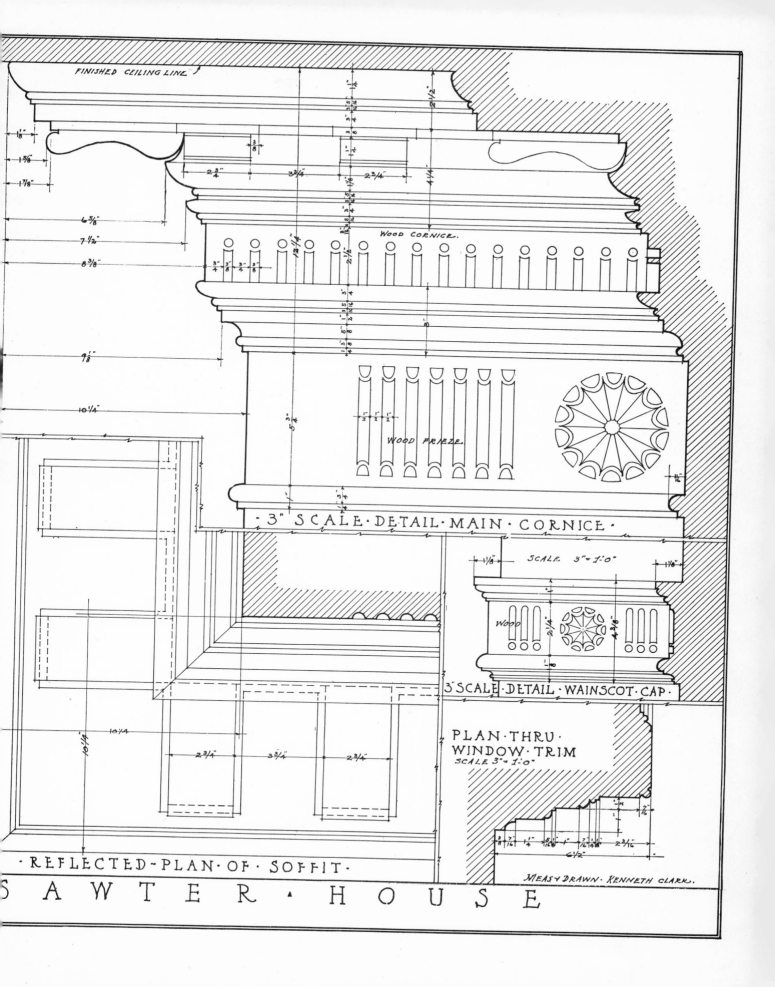

FINISHED CEILING LINE

WOOD CORNICE.

WOOD FRIEZE.

· 3" · SCALE · DETAIL · MAIN · CORNICE ·

SCALE 3" = 1'-0"

WOOD

3" SCALE · DETAIL · WAINSCOT · CAP ·

PLAN · THRU ·
WINDOW · TRIM
SCALE 3" = 1'-0"

· REFLECTED · PLAN · OF · SOFFIT ·

MEAS & DRAWN · KENNETH CLARK.

SAWTER · HOUSE

DETAIL OF MANTEL
IN DRAWING ROOM
SECOND FLOOR

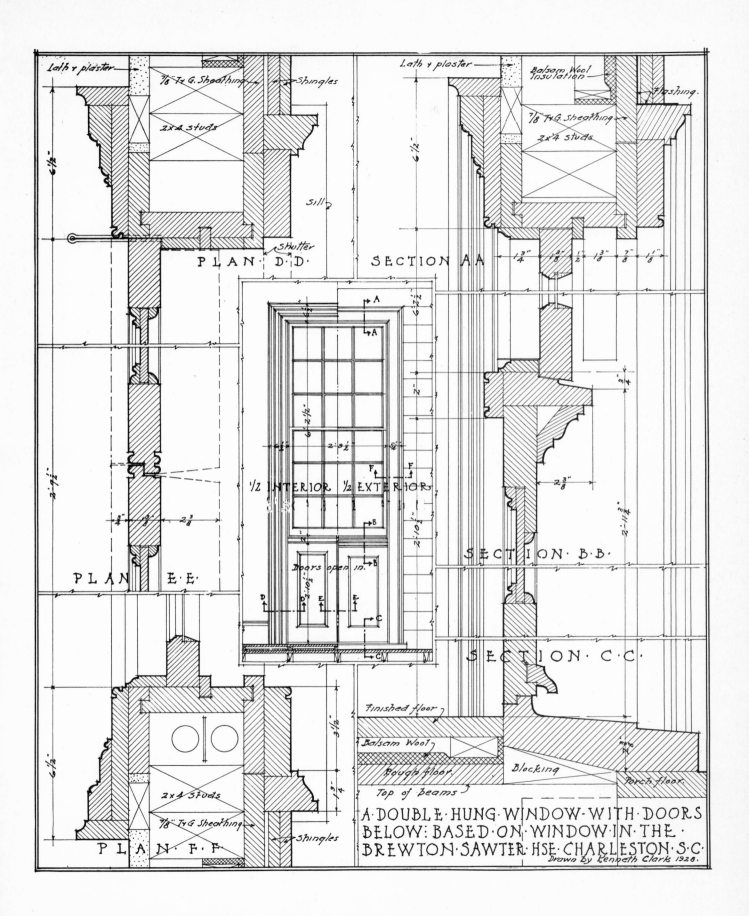

Lath + plaster

⅞" T+G Sheathing   Shingles

2×4 studs

6½"

Sill

PLAN·D·D·

shutter

Lath + plaster

Balsam Wool Insulation

Flashing.

6½"

⅞" T+G Sheathing

2×4 studs

SECTION·A·A·

1¾" ⅜" ½" 1⅜" ⅞" 1⅛"

6½"

2'-9½"

¾" ⅜" 2⅜"

PLAN·E·E·

½ INTERIOR   ½ EXTERIOR

6'-2½"

2'-9½"

Doors open in.

2'-10½"

A
A

2"

F
F

B
B

2'-10½"

D   D   E

E   C

C

SECTION·B·B·

3"/4"

2⅜"

2'-11¼"

SECTION·C·C·

3½"

1¾"

6½"

2×4 studs

⅞" T+G Sheathing

Shingles

PLAN·F·F·

Finished floor

Balsam Wool

Rough floor.

Blocking

Porch floor.

Top of beams

A·DOUBLE·HUNG·WINDOW·WITH·DOORS·
BELOW·BASED·ON·WINDOW·IN·THE·
BREWTON·SAWTER·HSE·CHARLESTON·S.C·
Drawn by Kenneth Clark 1928.

173

Corner in Ball Room

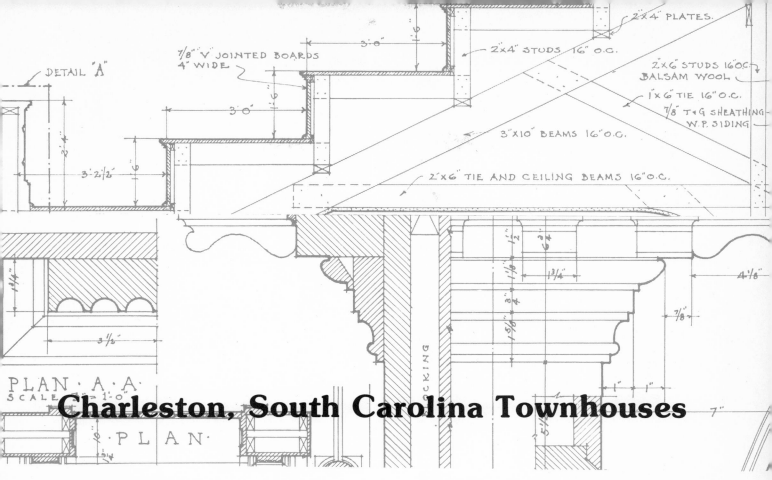

DETAIL "A"

7/8" V JOINTED BOARDS
4" WIDE

3'-0"

3'-2 1/2"

3'-0"

2 X 4 PLATES.

2 X 4 STUDS 16" O.C.

2 X 6 STUDS 16 O.C.
BALSAM WOOL

1 X 6 TIE 16" O.C.

7/8" T & G SHEATHING
W. P. SIDING

3" X 10" BEAMS 16" O.C.

2 X 6" TIE AND CEILING BEAMS 16" O.C.

4 1/8"

7/8"

BLOCKING

3 1/2"

7"

PLAN · A · A ·
SCALE

· PLAN ·

Charleston, South Carolina Townhouses

WHEN Josiah Quincy of Massachusetts visited Charleston in 1773, he was impressed by the material prosperity and hospitality of the people in the Carolina colony. In his published diary he wrote: "This town makes a beautiful appearance as you come up to it and in many respects a magnificent one. I can only say in general that in grandeur, splendor of buildings, decoration, equipages, numbers, commerce, shipping and indeed everything, it far surpasses all I ever saw, or can ever expect to see in America."

Charleston was isolated from its neighbors and the other sections of America. Dense forests separated the town from the other English Colonies and there were Indians on the West and Spaniards to the South. Commerce with the northern colonies was obstructed by the perils of the voyage around Cape Hatteras. These facts together with the character of the early settlers tended to make them independent in thought and action. One has a feeling that this independence exists even to-day. Surely a civilization and a sophistication have been created which are comparable to the most aristocratic of capitals. Charleston is the last remaining American city in which Madeira and Port and *noblesse oblige* are fully appreciated according to the finest traditions.

Just before Josiah Quincy's visit, four prominent citizens of Charleston, Robert MacKenzie, Edward Blake, George Kincaid and William Gibbes undertook to re-claim the salt marsh lands to the south of South Bay Street. It is interesting to note that even with the unlimited acreage of land available during the earliest days of colonization that a large part of the town is built on land reclaimed from the shores of the sea and rivers. The settlers were evidently intent upon making Charleston one of the few seaports in the world where a direct view of the ocean might be had from the city.

The walled in and filled up South Bay Street section was practically completed by 1772 and the reclaimed land was conveyed to Samuel Legaré and later to William Gibbes. The records show that both Gibbes and Blake built houses on the land included in this second conveyance soon after it came into Gibbes possession.

William Gibbes came direct to America from England. He took a prominent part in the life of Charleston and was active in behalf of the Colonies until the actual beginning of the hostilities with England. With native Americans living in London, he petitioned the King in favor of the Colonies and then at the opening of the Revolution escaped to Bermuda, and thence home.

The residence is supposed to have been built by Gibbes sometime before 1776. The records confirm this belief. The land on which the house now stands belonged to Gibbes and five years after his death in 1789 this house was sold to Mrs. Sarah Smithe for a consideration of £2500.

The ground floor or the basement of the Gibbes House is entered from the front at a level of a few inches above

FIRST FLOOR HALL

Newel and Stair Detail

Detail of West Door—Ball Room

West Doorway—Ball Room—Second Floor

the sidewalk. The foundation walls are built of brick and are about three feet thick. Flagstones, laid carefully, form the useful and lasting floor. The basement, as was the case in many houses of this period, was the center of the domestic activities of the household. Rooms for seamstresses, who worked under the supervision of the mistress of the house, play rooms for the children, storage rooms and rooms for the servants who were intimately connected with the family, were arranged here. Due to the good light and excellent ventilation this floor was ideally suited for its use.

The first floor is one full story above the ground, and is entered by a double flight of wide stone steps beginning at the street level on a slightly raised platform and meeting above on a broad stone landing. A wrought iron railing, simply designed, adds to the appearance of the facade. The front entrance itself is well designed and it is executed with a sympathetic feeling for detail and proportion, which characterizes the whole exterior of the house.

On ascending the front steps one is impressed with the feeling of privacy and security caused by the extreme height of the first or main floor above the sidewalk. It has been suggested that many houses in Charleston were built in this manner because the height of sea level prevented having a dry, excavated basement. There was no inexpensive and sure method of waterproofing at that time. However, in the case of the Gibbes house it is more reasonable to believe that the exterior design and the planning of the basement, so necessary to domestic life, were the governing motives in making the ceiling height of the ground floor so great.

It is evident that English-Georgian architecture influenced the character of the interior details. From the wide and impressive entrance hall on the first floor to the drawing room or "ball" room on the second floor, the work is executed in the elegant manner of the designers who were popular in the mother-country.

The first floor hall extends from the street entrance to the doorway from the garden approach—the entire length of the house. Unlike other hallways of the period, it is unbroken by an arch treatment. Columns and pilasters support the large span of the ceiling girder.

The stairway at the rear of the entrance hall is excellently proportioned. The graceful mahogany rail and the hand-wrought iron balusters add to the charm of the design. The stair landing forms a balcony across the full width of the rear of the hall from which a beautiful and unobstructed view can be had of the entrance and lower hall. The Palladian window on the landing gives

Detail of Façade

a splendid view of the garden and thoroughly lights the lower and upper halls.

The fine proportions, the refinement of detail and the wonderful material are fitting monuments to the work of the master designer and craftsman. In fact, all the carved woodwork was brought from England. The carved ornament has a freshness and an originality that gives it character and individuality without overstepping the bounds of good taste. All panelling and woodwork is put together with care, showing that the work was done by cabinet makers who took time to do things right and who spared no effort to get good results. All the wood wall panels seem to be in single pieces. The perfect state of preservation after over one hundred and fifty years of use is testimony as to the sincerity of con-

struction and the lasting qualities of the materials. It is of interest to note that only the plaster of some of the rooms was injured by the earthquake of 1886, although the chimneys still show cracks. The house passed through the wars of 1775 and 1861 without injury.

The ballroom on the second floor is particularly interesting. The excellent proportions of this room are most pleasing. Two doorways, one opening into a withdrawing-room and the other the entrance from the hall, are elegantly ornamented. The original and refreshing designs are all well executed. The ceiling with its Adam ornament is made of imported Italian stucco. This ceiling is the original. It has escaped injury and has never been changed or repaired in any way. Wood panelled walls, wide plank flooring in single pieces and a beauti-

THE WILLIAM GIBBES HOUSE, 64 SOUTH BAY STREET, CHARLESTON, SOUTH CAROLINA

Detail of North Door—Ball Room

Mantel in Ball Room

ful mantel complete this room. It would take hours of study to fully appreciate the proportions, the ornament and the execution of this wonderful design.

The second story room adjoining the ball room, which was probably once used as a "withdrawing" room and now as a bed room, has been carefully measured and the drawings illustrate the unusual treatment of the pilasters on the chimney breast, the marble mantel and the cornice with its elaborate "drop" ornament.

One of the most interesting features of this fine old house is its garden, protected from prying eyes by a brick wall and well placed shrubbery. The desire for privacy seems to have been a governing motive in the design of many of the town houses of Charleston. Within this garden filled with plants of almost tropical vegetation, many of which are native to South Carolina, are found servants' quarters, a kitchen and storage space. The kitchen is equipped with a huge fireplace and a Dutch oven. Wide pine flooring—scrubbed white—gives the impression of cleanliness and domesticity associated with the colored servants of the Old South.

The Gibbes house and dependencies bear witness that the owner was not only a man of wealth, but also of culture and good taste.

This town house, inside and out, shows careful and intelligent study. Sometimes in our haste to praise all things foreign, we forget the great wealth of material we have at home. Our old houses are honest and sincere, inasmuch as they were designed and built to fill a local need. The Charleston houses are, it seems, particularly adaptable as an inspiration for the designing and building of the modern American home.

Front Room—First Floor

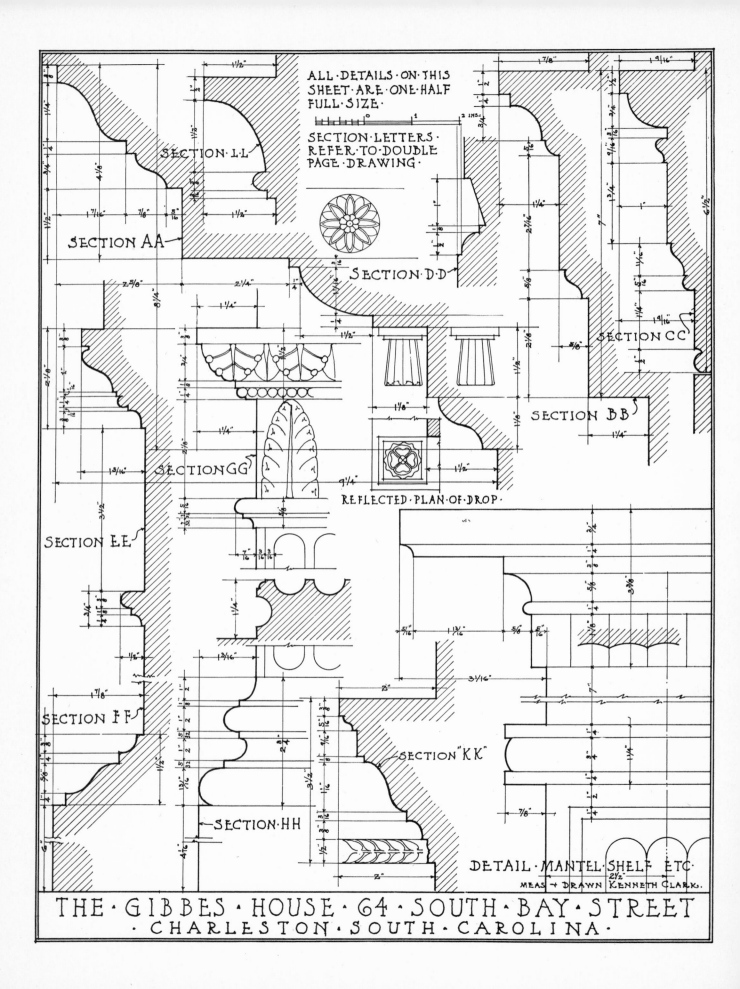

ALL·DETAILS·ON·THIS
SHEET·ARE·ONE·HALF
FULL·SIZE·

SECTION·LETTERS·
REFER·TO·DOUBLE
PAGE·DRAWING·

SECTION·LL

SECTION·AA

SECTION·DD

SECTION·CC

SECTION·BB

SECTION·GG

SECTION·EE

REFLECTED·PLAN·OF·DROP·

SECTION·FF

SECTION "KK"

SECTION·HH

DETAIL·MANTEL·SHELF·ETC·
MEAS + DRAWN KENNETH CLARK.

THE·GIBBES·HOUSE·64·SOUTH·BAY·STREET
·CHARLESTON·SOUTH·CAROLINA·

East Wall—Southwest Room—Second Floor

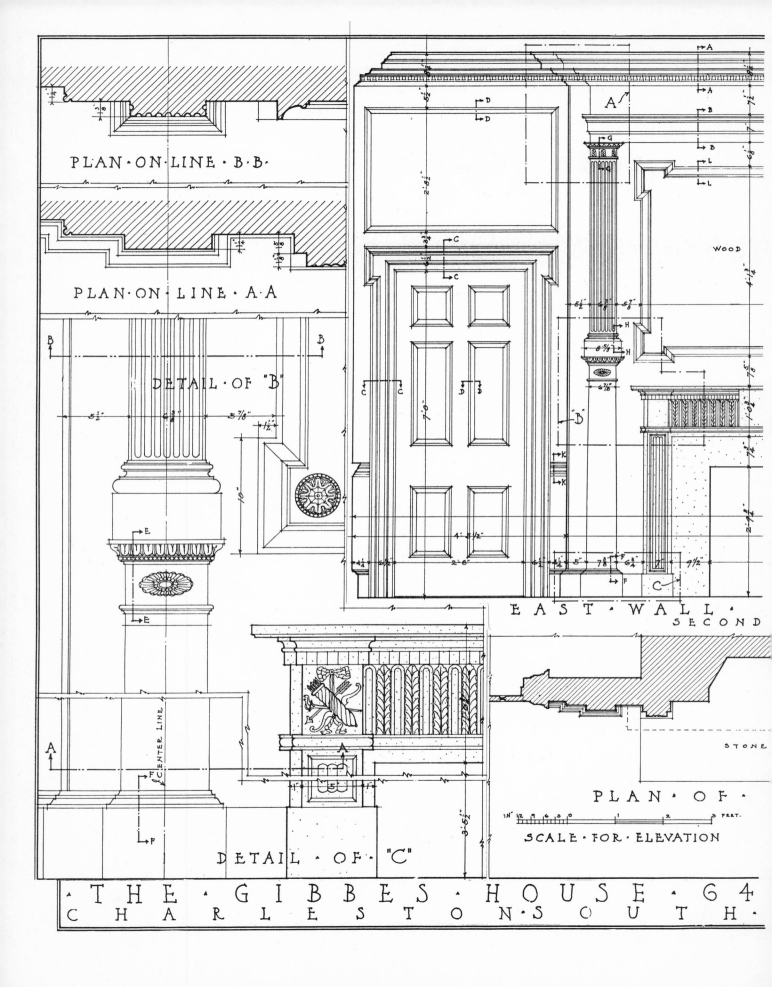

PLAN·ON·LINE·B·B

PLAN·ON·LINE·A·A

DETAIL·OF·"B"

WOOD

EAST·WALL·

SECOND

STONE

PLAN·OF·

DETAIL·OF·"C"

SCALE·FOR·ELEVATION

·THE·GIBBES·HOUSE·64·
CHARLESTON·SOUTH·

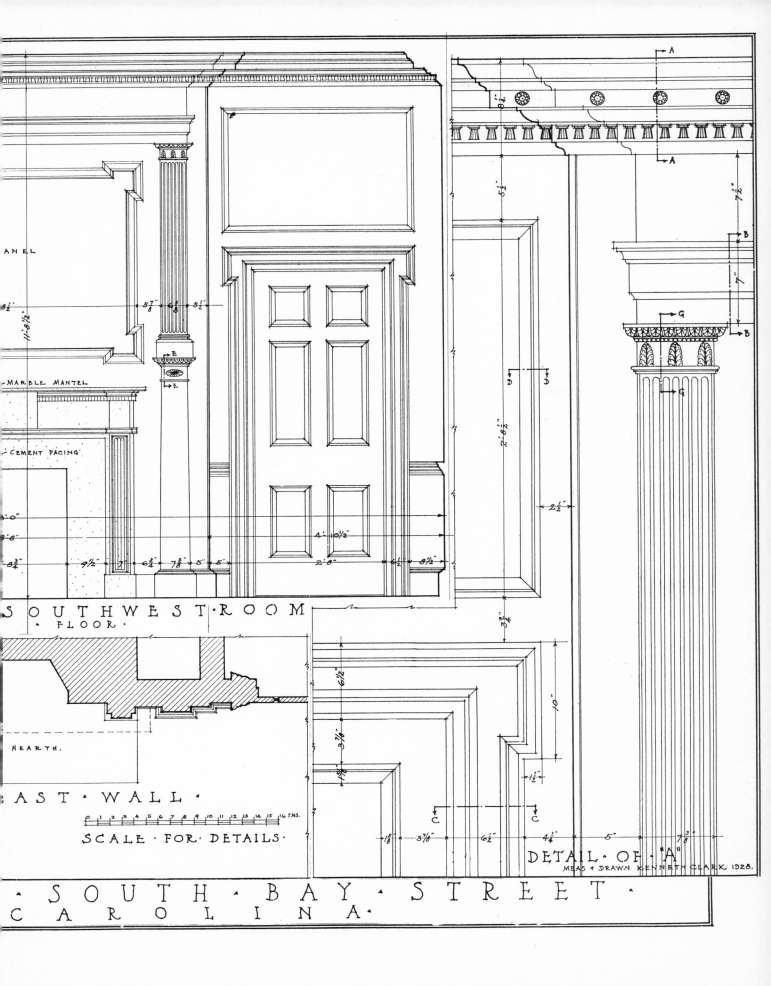

AHEL

−MARBLE MANTEL

CEMENT FACING

HEARTH.

SOUTHWEST ROOM
FLOOR.

EAST WALL.

SCALE FOR DETAILS.

DETAIL OF "A"
MEAS + DRAWN KENNETH CLARK 1928.

SOUTH BAY STREET
CAROLINA.

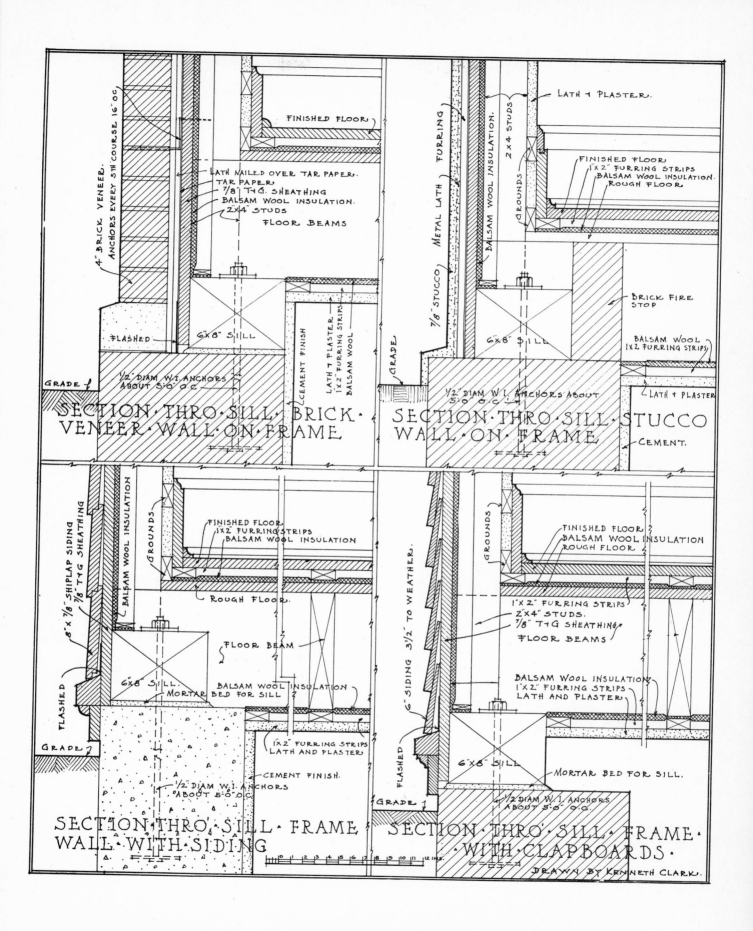

SECTION·THRO·SILL·BRICK·
VENEER·WALL·ON·FRAME

SECTION·THRO·SILL·STUCCO
WALL·ON·FRAME

SECTION·THRO·SILL·FRAME·
WALL·WITH·SIDING

SECTION·THRO·SILL·FRAME·
WITH·CLAPBOARDS·

DRAWN·BY·KENNETH·CLARK·

Section Thro Sill Brick Veneer Wall on Frame:

4" BRICK VENEER.
ANCHORS EVERY 5TH COURSE 16" O.C.
FINISHED FLOOR
LATH NAILED OVER TAR PAPER.
TAR PAPER.
7/8" T+G. SHEATHING.
BALSAM WOOL INSULATION.
2×4" STUDS
FLOOR BEAMS
FLASHED
6"×8" SILL
GRADE
1/2" DIAM. W.I. ANCHORS ABOUT 5'-0" O.C.
CEMENT FINISH
LATH + PLASTER
1×2" FURRING STRIPS
BALSAM WOOL

Section Thro Sill Stucco Wall on Frame:

LATH + PLASTER.
7/8" STUCCO. METAL LATH. FURRING
BALSAM WOOL INSULATION
2×4 STUDS
GROUNDS
FINISHED FLOOR
1"×2" FURRING STRIPS
BALSAM WOOL INSULATION.
ROUGH FLOOR
BRICK FIRE STOP
BALSAM WOOL 1×2 FURRING STRIPS
GRADE
6"×8" SILL
1/2" DIAM W.I. ANCHORS ABOUT 5'-0" O.C.
LATH + PLASTER
CEMENT.

Section Thro Sill Frame Wall With Siding:

8"×7/8" SHIPLAP SIDING
7/8" T+G SHEATHING
BALSAM WOOL INSULATION
GROUNDS
FINISHED FLOOR
1×2 FURRING STRIPS
BALSAM WOOL INSULATION
ROUGH FLOOR
FLOOR BEAM
FLASHED
6"×8" SILL.
MORTAR BED FOR SILL
BALSAM WOOL INSULATION
1×2" FURRING STRIPS
LATH AND PLASTER
GRADE
1/2" DIAM W.I. ANCHORS ABOUT 5'-0" O.C.
CEMENT FINISH.

Section Thro Sill Frame With Clapboards:

GROUNDS
FINISHED FLOOR
BALSAM WOOL INSULATION
ROUGH FLOOR
6" SIDING 3 1/2 TO WEATHER.
1"×2" FURRING STRIPS
2"×4" STUDS.
7/8" T+G SHEATHING
FLOOR BEAMS
BALSAM WOOL INSULATION
1"×2" FURRING STRIPS
LATH AND PLASTER
FLASHED
6"×8" SILL
MORTAR BED FOR SILL.
GRADE
1/2" DIAM W.I. ANCHORS ABOUT 5'-0" O.C.

10 1 2 3 4 5 6 7 8 9 10 11 12 INS.

Number 14 Legaré Street

THE EDWARDS-SMYTH HOUSE, CHARLESTON, SOUTH CAROLINA

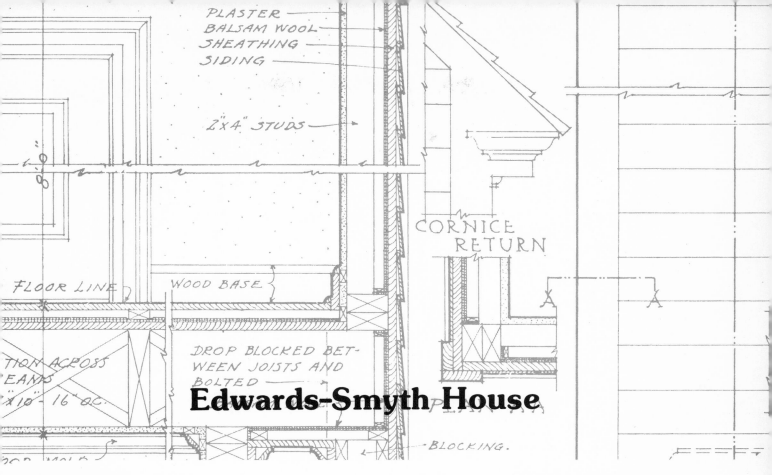

PLASTER
BALSAM WOOL
SHEATHING
SIDING

2"X4" STUDS

CORNICE
RETURN

FLOOR LINE

WOOD BASE

TION ACROSS
EAMS
"X10 - 16 OC.

DROP BLOCKED BET-
WEEN JOISTS AND
BOLTED

BLOCKING.

Edwards-Smyth House

IN A CITY of interesting buildings the Edwards-Smyth house is one of the most distinguished. While in every way the outgrowth of local, climatic and social requirements, it has more-over, that flavor of cosmopolitan sophistication that is ever an attribute of good breeding. While essentially a Charleston House, it could take its place without embarrassment in Blackheath, London, or in Lansdowne Place, Bath, where its later Georgian kinship would at once receive recognition. Designed for a sub-tropical climate where heat lingers and winter is only a pleasant interlude, it rises from a high arcaded basement above the spacious gardens and towers up three lofty stories to a roomy garret. No breeze can blow in from the harbor without entering one of its many tall windows, while the long piazzas shade the chambers from the ardors of the too intense sun of summer noons.

The servants' quarters are detached at a convenient distance from the house and bespeak a social order that provided gracious, if not always efficient, domestic service.

Thus far it is local and follows well established precedent. It is the thoroughly studied assurance displayed in combining all of the elements, the piazzas, the gates, the fence, the dependencies and the garden into a unified scheme that mark it as the work of more than the amateur. Many other houses in Charleston have employed all of these elements but none have combined them more happily. Let us consider the fence and gate-

way. If the house were not of such towering proportions it would be overbalanced by such monumental gates and posts, but the unity is sustained by using the same brickwork as in the house and preserving the same rather small scale throughout all of the detail. The gates combine the use of wood and wrought iron in a rather unusual but successful manner. The doorway, though simple, gains emphasis by being framed by two quadrants of wrought iron grilles and is approached by a short flight of marble steps curving outward in the most welcoming gesture. Within the door the steps continue up to the first story piazza.

The long many storied piazza is one of the most characteristic features of the houses of Charleston and gives the town much of its individuality. Seldom however, do they tie in with the architectural composition and in most cases are frankly a compromise between correct design and convenience. In this case the matter has been handled with the greatest tact. A screen of brick work has been carried across the street end which ties it to the house and serves as a setting for the doorway. This screen is finished by the cornice of the first story piazza. Looking through the fence we see repeated in two tiers the prolonged rhythm of eight widely spaced and very slender columns bearing very flat segmental arches. This type of arcade occurs frequently in Charleston and on one nearby plantation, but as far as the writer's observation goes, does not appear in quite this form in other American towns of this period, nor does there seem to be any English or continental precedent for its use. It is, however, obviously Adam in its inspiration and recalls those segmental vaults and arches that occur at Sion House and other Adam buildings which were in turn derived from vaults found at Pompeii, and in those charming stuccoed grottoes in the via Latina near Rome. These arch forms are not structural of course, but are only simulated in wood. However, the grace of line achieved, justifies this piece of architectural fiction. The capitals of the columns are typically Adam with a single row of slender laurel leaves about the neck. The banister rail is kept as simple and delicate in scale as possible in order that it may not interrupt the clean lines of the columns.

The brickwork of the house, while restrained, is worthy of note. The corners of the front are accented by long and short quoins of projecting brickwork and the stories are marked off in like manner by flat belt courses. In the flat arches over the windows, the bricks are ground so as to come to a straight line at the bottom and top and the mortar joint is kept to a uniform width. One other refinement has been introduced. As the Carolina "grey brick" is hand made and quite uneven along its edges, the joints have been filled with mortar of the color of the brick and then a narrow tooled joint has been worked in of white mortar. This narrow white line contrasts agreeably with the dull rust color of the brick.

Entering the stair hall from the middle of the piazza, we find that the plan of the building is quite simple, consisting of two large rooms on each floor separated by the hall. There is an addendum of smaller rooms at the back

but this is obviously of later construction than the house and is of no special interest.

The stairway begins its flight on the left side of the hall and continues upward to the garret without a break in the continuity of the mahogany handrail. This rail is carried on delicate wooden spokes of rectangular section and stiffened at intervals by iron rods of the same appearance as the wooden spokes so that no newel posts are required. The hall ceiling has an ornamental plaster treatment consisting of a centerpiece of garlands of husks and radiating laurel leaves, and a flat band on the soffit of the stairs against the wall of a vine motif which is continued up through the second story hall. The rooms overlooking the street on both the first and second floors are given the more elaborate treatment, yet the back rooms are sufficiently ornate to make it quite evident that all four rooms were intended for the reception and entertainment of guests, the four rooms on the third and fourth stories being reserved for bedchambers. As the four main rooms are rather similar let us consider only the rear dining room on the first story and front drawing room on the second floor. In the dining room the rather chaste mantle of flat pilasters and garlanded frieze is set between two doors opening into closets formed by the chimney breasts. On the garden side between a door and a window we find an arched and panelled recess, the proper setting in which to enshrine the sideboard. Opposite the fireplace are two tall recessed windows overlooking the piazza. The architrave of all the windows

Drawing Room, First Floor

ENTRANCE GATEWAY AND FENCE
THE EDWARDS·SMYTH HOUSE
14 LEGARÉ STREET
CHARLESTON, SOUTH CAROLINA

MEASURED DRAWINGS *from*
The George F. Lindsay Collection

GARDEN SIDE—LOOKING TOWARD THE STREET

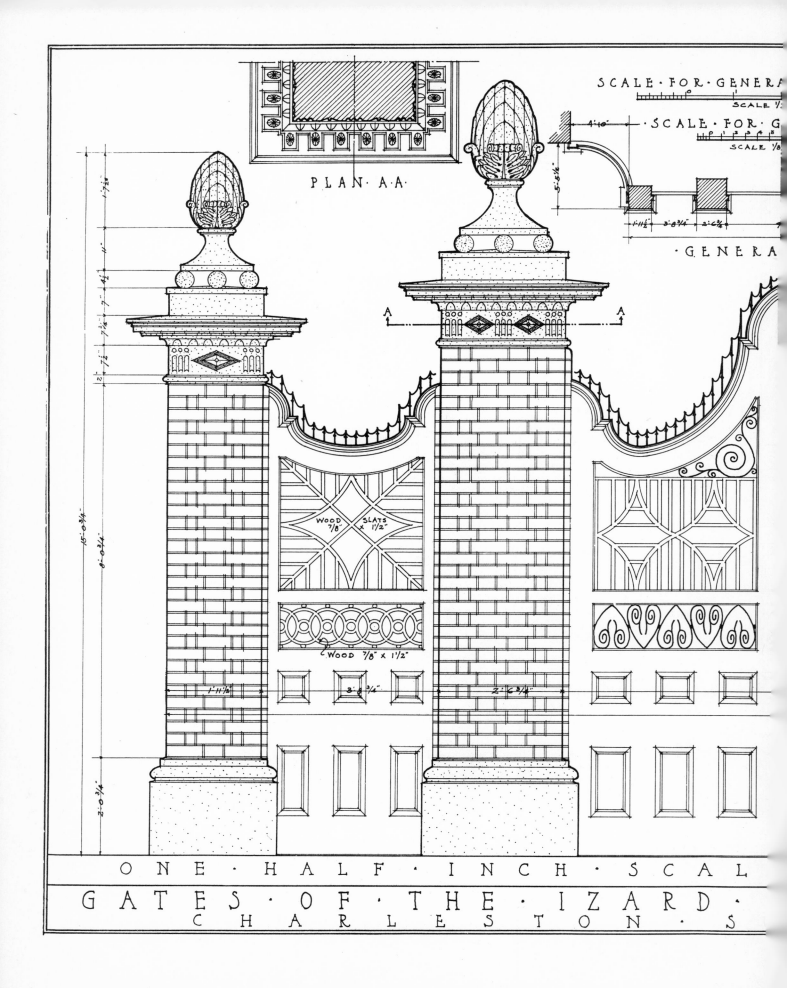

PLAN · A·A·

SCALE · FOR · GENERA

SCALE · FOR · G

· GENERA

WOOD
SLATS
7/8"
X 1 1/2"

WOOD 7/8" X 1 1/2"

· ONE · HALF · INCH · SCAL

GATES · OF · THE · IZARD ·

CHARLESTON · S

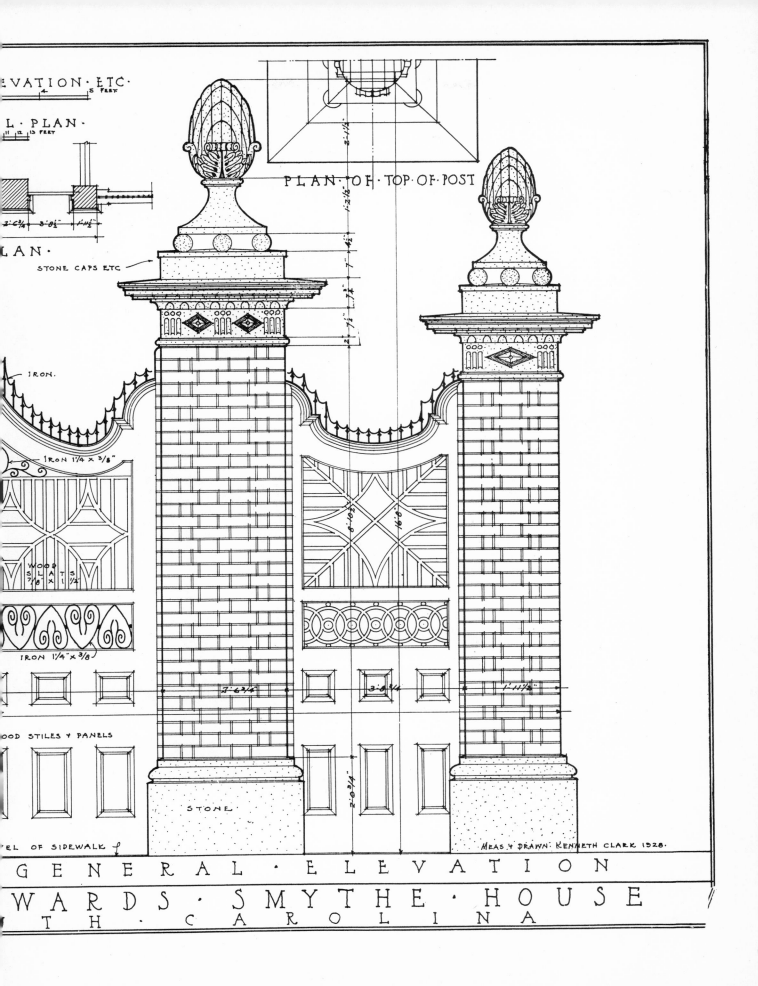

VATION · ETC.

L · PLAN ·

LAN ·

STONE CAPS ETC

PLAN · OF · TOP · OF · POST

IRON.

IRON 1 1/4 X 3/8"

WOOD
SLATS
7/8 X 1 1/2

IRON 1 1/4" X 3/8"

OOD STILES & PANELS

EL OF SIDEWALK

STONE

MEAS. & DRAWN KENNETH CLARK 1928.

G E N E R A L · E L E V A T I O N

WARDS · SMYTHE · HOUSE

TH · C A R O L I N A

comes just below the bottom plaster frieze and is enriched only with a band of simple reeding. The same
architrave is carried around the door leading into the
hall. All of the windows throughout the house have inside shutters that fold back into the jambs of the windows and show as panels on the face. There is a panelled
wainscot about three feet high extending around the
room. The band in the wainscot cap is enriched with
swags indicated by short incised lines placed close together. Above the wainscot the plaster walls continue
unbroken. There is a very flat plaster cornice at the ceiling with a plaster frieze below made interesting by an
alternating rhythm of a group of channels and rosettes.

In the second floor drawing room a much more ornate
treatment has been carried out. The mantle has engaged
columns of bold projection and the frieze has garlands
and baskets of fruits and flowers, scrolls and attenuated
rinceau while the mantel shelf curves outward in the cen-
tre and inward at the ends. The hall door has not only
an enriched architrave but a frieze and a cornice as well
and is balanced symmetrically by a false door which if
opened would plunge us down the stair well. The wainscot is similar to that in the dining room but it is in the
plaster work that the greatest enrichment has been lavished. The centerpiece covers a considerable area of the
ceiling and consists of six garlands of husks surrounding
a circular band of alternating anthemion and palmettes
about a huge rosette of wind blown acanthus leaves. The
plaster cornice has a frieze bearing another variant of
the anthemion motif while on the ceiling near the cornice are bands of countersunk reeding interrupted at regular intervals by enriched squares. The general effect of
this room is much more gay and sumptuous than the
dining room.

The bedrooms on the third floor have garlanded mantels, panelled wainscot, simple trim for doors and windows and very plain plaster cornices. The garret rooms
are without fireplaces but are plastered and neatly
trimmed, even on this story the windows have carefully
fitted folding shutters in the window jambs. The workmanship throughout the house is uniform in general
period and character.

Behind the house stands the kitchen with servants'
quarters above and further to the rear is the stable and
coach house with dormer rooms under the roof for the

Detail of Entrance—14 Legaré Street

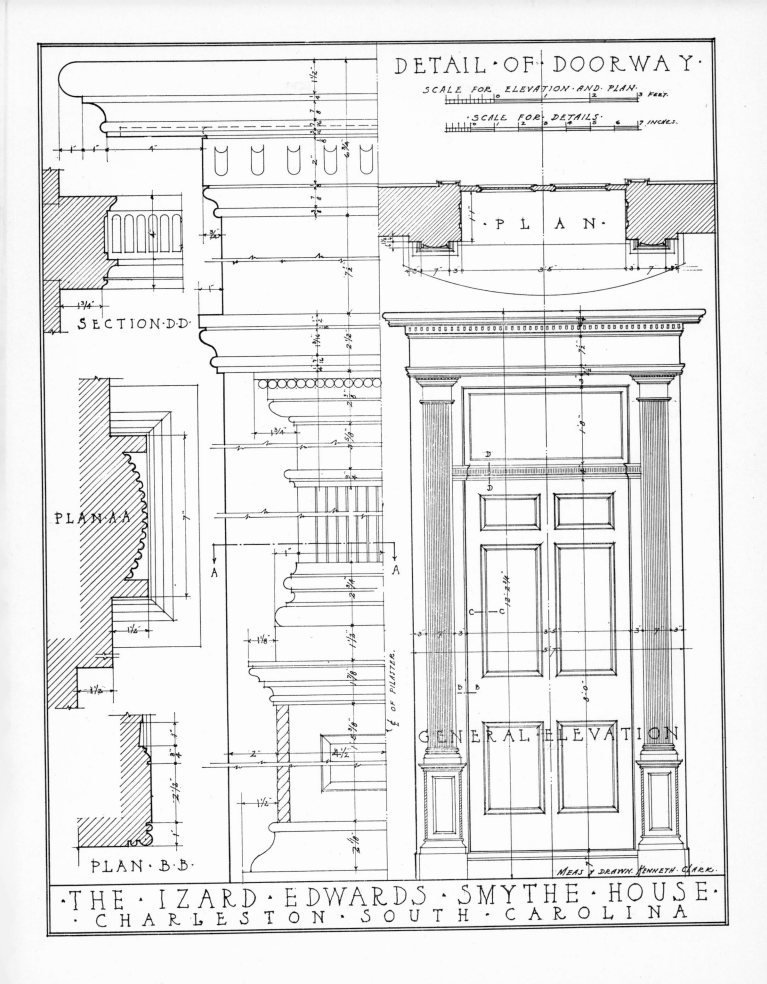

DETAIL·OF·DOORWAY·

SCALE FOR ELEVATION·AND·PLAN·

·SCALE FOR DETAILS·

·PLAN·

SECTION·D·D·

PLAN·A·A·

GENERAL·ELEVATION

PLAN·B·B·

MEAS'y DRAWN. KENNETH CLARK.

·THE·IZARD·EDWARDS·SMYTHE·HOUSE·
·CHARLESTON·SOUTH·CAROLINA·

The Doorway into the Second Floor Hall

stable boys. These service buildings are separated from the garden by a screen of slender Tuscan columns with parapet walls between bearing panels of light wooden railings. Within the garden is a tiny octagonal tea house with a pagoda-like roof. Rising in the midst of oleanders, spice bays, pomegranates and spikenards, it strikes an exotic note in harmony with the sub-tropical setting.

Documentary evidence as to the dates at which the property has changed title is available but in the lack of more specific information these dates are inconclusive in determining when the house now standing was built.

The property consists of two lots. The original grant was made to Richard Philips in 1694 and was later conveyed to Ralph Izard. In 1767 Ralph Izard conveyed to Barnwell Elliott. In 1784 the Master in Chancery conveys to Benj. Waller "all that certain brick residence and lot lately belonging to Ralph Izard." In 1816 George Edwards bought a brick house and lot 52' x 270' for $20,000, and in 1818 the southern lot including a wooden house for $4,000.

The character of the house is most obviously post-revolutionary as comparison with authentically dated Charleston houses will show. Owing to the very adverse economic conditions that prevailed in Charleston for several years after the close of the Revolution, it is most unlikely that a building of this magnificence should have been erected between the evacuation of the town by the British in 1782, and 1784 when it passed to Benj. Waller. It is most improbable therefore, that the brick building on the property that came to Waller is the present dwelling. Now Waller owned the property for some thirty-two years from 1784 to 1816 and the writer is of the opinion that it was during this period in the revival of prosperity that this fine house was built. However, it is to George Edwards that we owe the iron fence, gates and pillars as is evidenced by his initials G. E. in the grilles flanking the doorway and by the additional fact that he bought the southern lot making the complete fence possible. The fifty-two feet of the original lot ended at the south in the middle of the coach gate. In the house there is no evidence of remodelling or patching together of work of different periods, so that the building of the house was carefully planned *de nouveau* and completed at one time while the same mode dominated. Even the gates, while later than the house, are much of the same period and suggest that they were built not many years later. While the above cannot be substantiated by documentary evidence it will doubtless satisfy most architects as plausible and the lack of specific dates will not deter their enjoyment of this very delightful building.

DRAWING ROOM CORNICE, SECOND FLOOR

Mantel in Drawing Room, Second Floor

DINING ROOM MANTEL

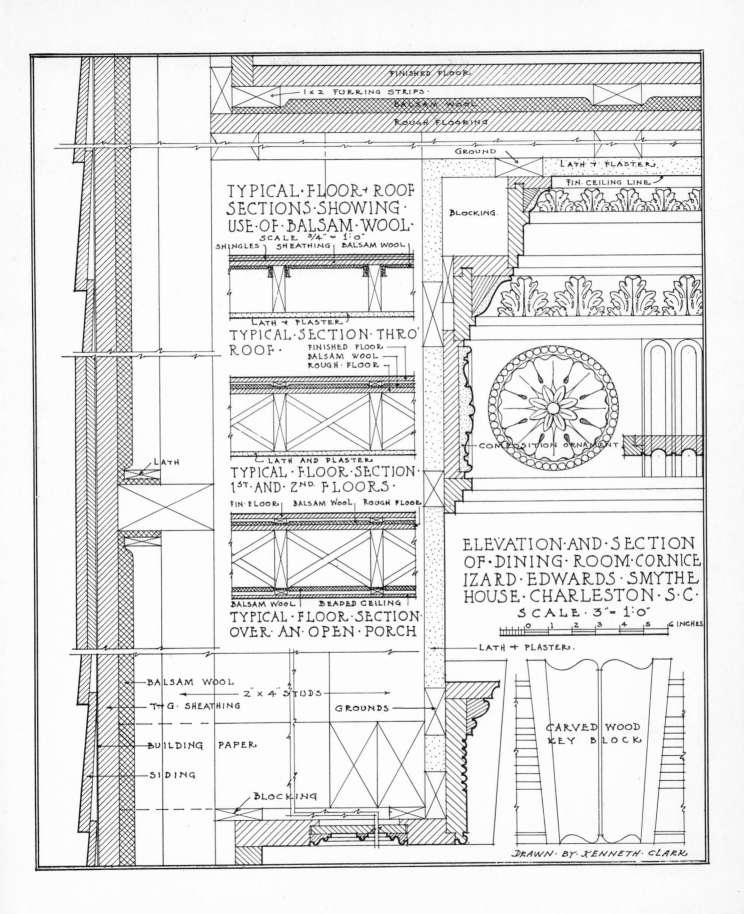

TYPICAL·FLOOR·ROOF
SECTIONS·SHOWING·
USE·OF·BALSAM·WOOL·
SCALE 3/4" = 1:0"

SHINGLES   SHEATHING   BALSAM WOOL

LATH + PLASTER

TYPICAL·SECTION·THRO'
ROOF·

FINISHED FLOOR
BALSAM WOOL
ROUGH·FLOOR

LATH AND PLASTER

TYPICAL·FLOOR·SECTION·
1ST·AND·2ND·FLOORS·

FIN·FLOOR   BALSAM WOOL   ROUGH FLOOR

BALSAM WOOL   BEADED CEILING

TYPICAL·FLOOR·SECTION·
OVER·AN·OPEN·PORCH

BALSAM WOOL
← 2"x 4" STUDS →
T+G· SHEATHING   GROUNDS

BUILDING PAPER

SIDING

LATH

BLOCKING

FINISHED FLOOR.
1x2 FURRING STRIPS·
BALSAM WOOL
ROUGH FLOORING

GROUND   LATH + PLASTER.

BLOCKING.   FIN. CEILING LINE

COMPOSITION ORNAMENT

ELEVATION·AND·SECTION·
OF·DINING·ROOM·CORNICE·
IZARD·EDWARDS·SMYTHE·
HOUSE·CHARLESTON·S·C·
SCALE· 3"= 1:0"
0 1 2 3 4 5 6 INCHES

LATH + PLASTER.

CARVED WOOD
KEY BLOCK

DRAWN·BY·KENNETH·CLARK

SERVANTS'
QUARTERS

STABLE AND
COACH HOUSE

Gate Posts and Fence

End of Coach House and Fence

DOORWAY—104 TRADD STREET,
CHARLESTON, SOUTH CAROLINA

Erected before 1772 by Col. John Stuart

SECOND
FLOOR
PLAN

ONE-EIGHTH OF AN INCH EQUALS ONE FOOT

THREE FOURTHS OF AN INCH EQUALS ONE FOOT

THREE INCHES EQUALS ONE FOOT

CORNICE
AT MAIN
ENTRANCE

FRITZ

CUBAGE

'A'

45 X 24 X
29½' = 31 860 cu. ft.

CELLAR

A	MAIN HOUSE	31,860
B	KITCHEN WING	7,182
C	GARAGE WING	7,733
D	LIVING PORCH	864
		540
		60
G	GATE WALL	100
H	DORM'R	66
	TOTAL	48,405 cu. ft.

'D'
25 % OF
12' X 24'
X 12' =
864 cu.ft.

MAIN ENTRANCE

Charleston, South Carolina Doorways

THOUGH Architecture is unquestionably the most "human" of all the arts, it is less understood by the layman and the public generally than either music, painting or literature. This is perhaps because the Architect is restricted in his design to materials and their use in ways that make it supremely difficult to express beauty of the ordinarily recognizable variety. His beauty must be that of proportion, spacing and contrast and his picture has no direct "subject" to intrigue the mind of the beholder into romantic speculation and enthusiasm.

The part of the exterior design of the house that lends itself most easily as an appeal to popular appreciation is the doorway or "Frontispiece" and on this the designer usually lavishes his greatest skill.

The doorway as a detail can give the key and accent to a facade and can reflect the spirit of the builder or the owner. It may be imbued with the characteristics of dignity, simplicity, pretentiousness, etc., that we usu-

ally associate with human beings, and thus subtly express to the passer-by what lies within—whether it be wealth or poverty, the warmth of hospitality or the chill of aloofness.

The development of our Early American Architecture can be traced more clearly, and with less deviation from the true path, by its doorways, than through any other detail. For in the doorway, the index of the style of the house and its period are most clearly indicated. Starting with the Jacobian influence apparent in the 17th Century examples, and on through the Renaissance, Georgian and Greek Revival Periods, there is a distinct chronological path that can be followed by the investigator.

Charleston, South Carolina, offers some interesting examples that are in a way unique as to scheme and execution. The custom of placing the main entrance of the house at the street end of a side piazza or gallery, thus giving admission to the "Estate" with an entirely separate door leading from the porch to the interior of

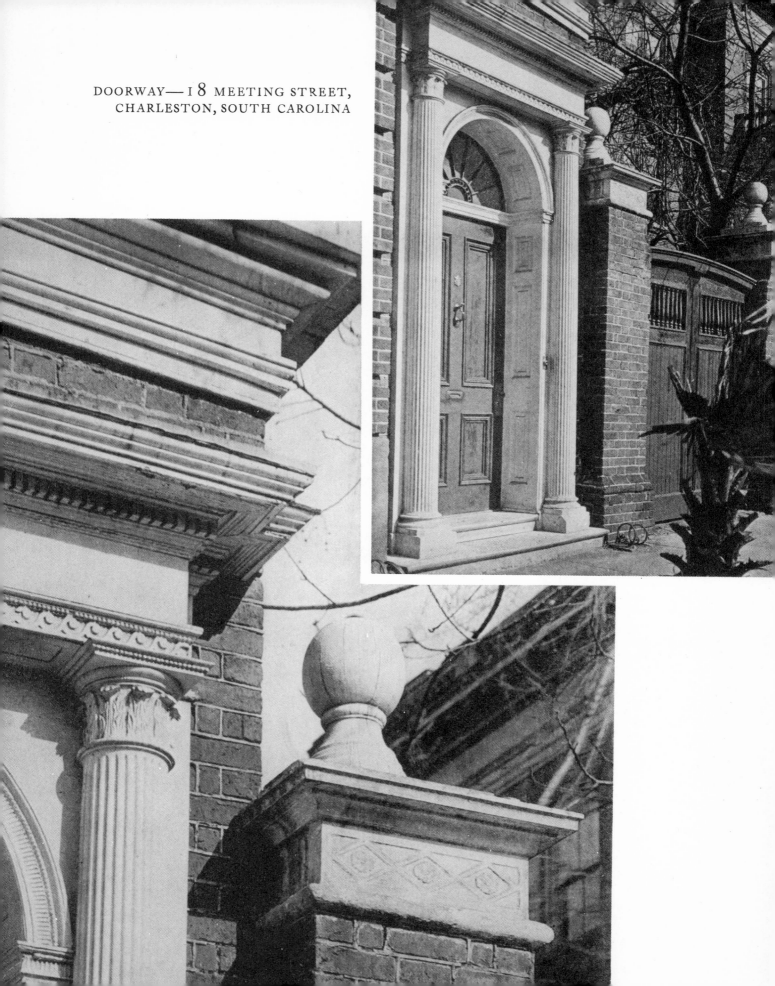

DOORWAY—18 MEETING STREET,
CHARLESTON, SOUTH CAROLINA

the house proper, has much to recommend it under the circumstances and habits of the families of Charleston who created a city of beautiful houses and gardens that are unsurpassed in our early work. The casual visitor on entering through the street door could be received on the porch out of the gaze of the passer-by and there entertained or having passed inspection could be welcomed to the hospitality of the house itself. Lucky is the person who comes within the latter category, for the privilege of enjoying Charleston hospitality is not lightly conferred, but once given is a thing to be remembered. Here perhaps the spirit of the old South has its firmest present hold, not the South of sentimental story book variety, but the true South of culture, refinement and solidity that has been engendered by years of association of one group of families in one environment who are homogenious enough to cast off influences that would corrupt their culture and tradition.

The oldest examples of Charleston houses, still standing, date back to about 1750, but of the earlier examples few are left. The period of her architects' greatest achievement was from about 1760 to the Revolution and her finest houses date from within this space of about sixteen years. While the type of plan and the general scheme of the larger houses are more or less similar, the exterior designs display an ingenious use of materials, knowingly arranged. Perhaps what is most apparent is the infinite variety of doorway motives which were used during both the early and later periods of Charleston's architectural growth. Many of these frontispieces undoubtedly perished in the fires and earthquakes that have taken toll of her buildings in the past, but enough remain to establish the fact that her early designers were fully competent and have left to us a heritage that cannot be ignored. Charleston is one of the most important architectural shrines in America.

DOORWAY—KING STREET,
CHARLESTON, SOUTH CAROLINA

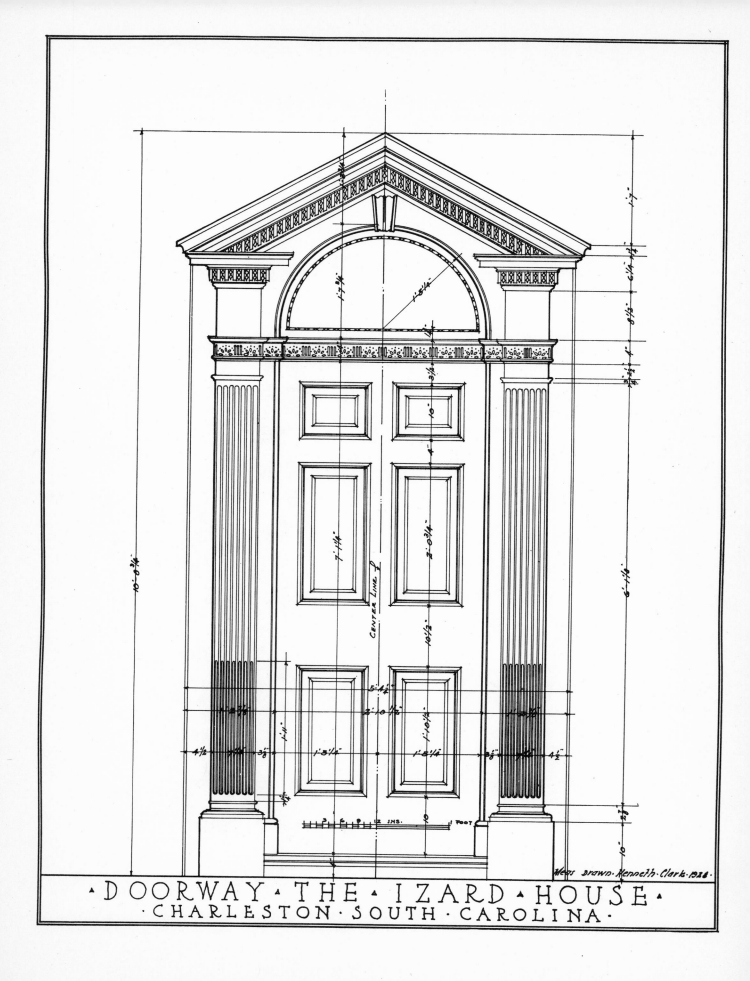

· D O O R W A Y · T H E · I Z A R D · H O U S E ·
· C H A R L E S T O N · S O U T H · C A R O L I N A ·

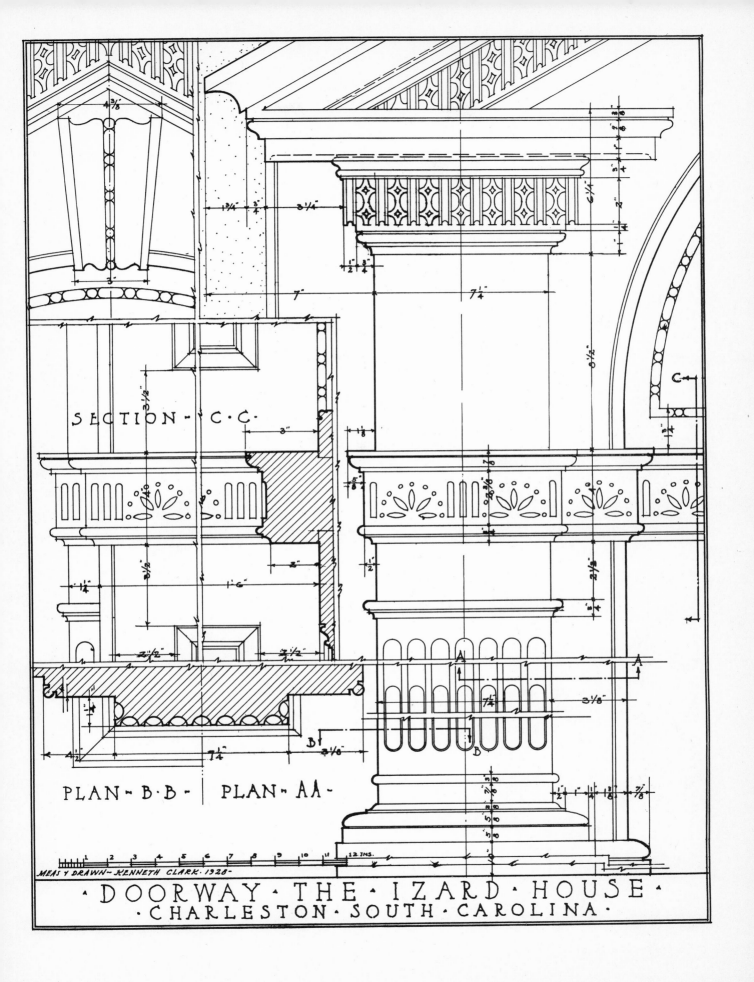

SECTION - C·C·

PLAN - B·B· | PLAN - AA ·

MEAS'D DRAWN ~ KENNETH CLARK · 1928 ~

· D O O R W A Y · T H E · I Z A R D · H O U S E ·
· C H A R L E S T O N · S O U T H · C A R O L I N A ·

THE RALPH IZARD HOUSE
110 BROAD STREET
CHARLESTON, SOUTH CAROLINA

MEASURED DRAWINGS *from*
The George F. Lindsay Collection

DOORWAY
110 BROAD STREET,
CHARLESTON,
SOUTH CAROLINA

Erected before 1757 by Ralph Izard

DOORWAY
3OI EAST BAY, SOUTH,
CHARLESTON,
SOUTH CAROLINA

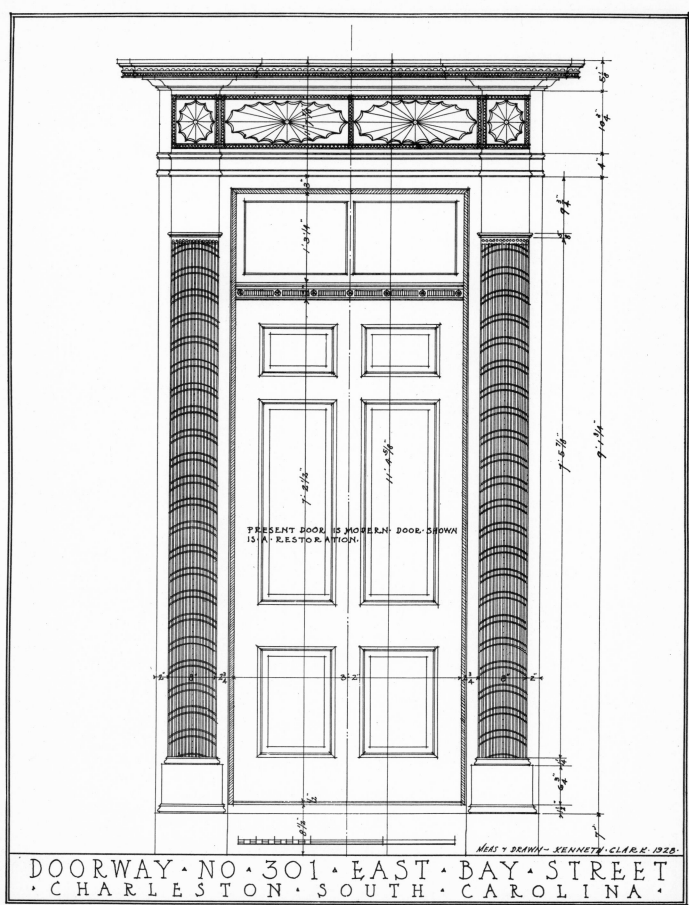

PRESENT DOOR IS MODERN. DOOR SHOWN
IS A RESTORATION.

MEAS. & DRAWN~ KENNETH·CLARK·1928·

DOORWAY·NO·301·EAST·BAY·STREET
·CHARLESTON·SOUTH·CAROLINA·

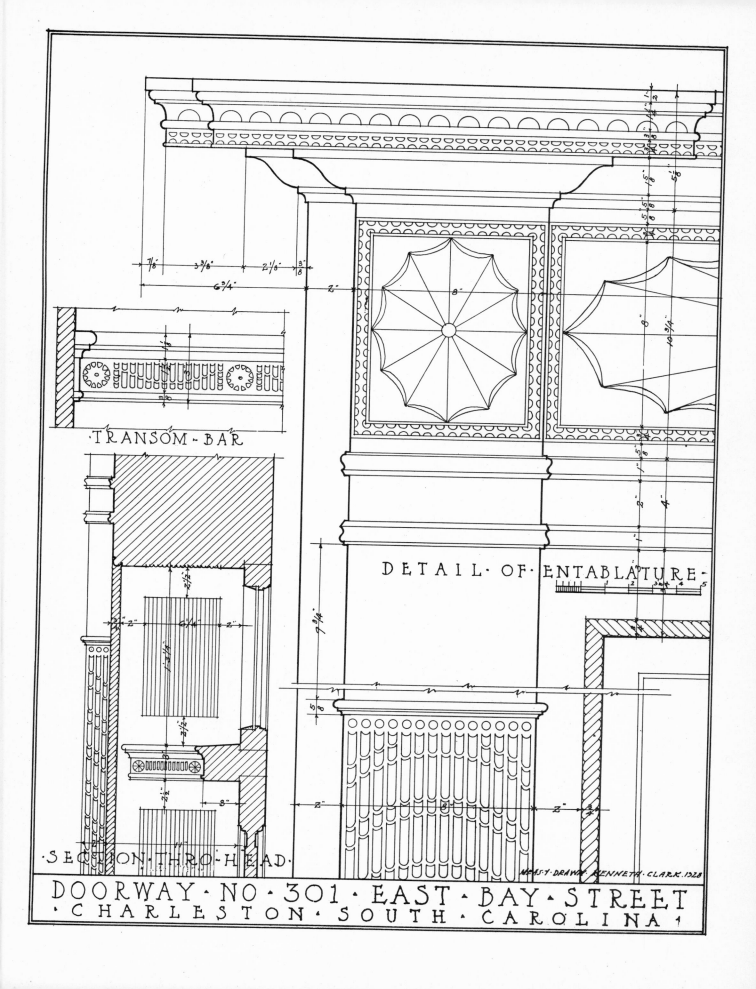

TRANSOM · BAR

DETAIL · OF · ENTABLATURE ·

· SECTION · THRO · HEAD ·

MEAS'T · DRAWN · KENNETH · CLARK · 1928

DOORWAY · NO · 301 · EAST · BAY · STREET
· CHARLESTON · SOUTH · CAROLINA ·

DOORWAY—39 SOUTH BATTERY,
CHARLESTON, SOUTH CAROLINA

A· DOORWAY·
BASED· ON· THE·
DOORWAY· OF· THE·
MAGWOOD· HOUSE·
AT· 39· SOUTH·
BATTERY·
CHARLESTON·
SOUTH· CAROLINA·

½· PLAN· A· A·

· P L A N ·

· G E N E R A L · E L E V A T I O N ·

· BLOCKING ·

· BLOCKING ·

· D E T A I L · E L E V A T I O N ·

· DRAWN· KENNETH· CLARK· 1928·

213

SPRING-HOUSE AND DAIRY, ESTATE OF GOODLOE HARPER,
BALTIMORE COUNTY, MARYLAND.   Built about 1800.

Early American Dependencies

LIVING in the country a hundred years or more ago was by no means the simple matter that it is to-day. The farmer generally raised most of his own living on his own farm; he didn't buy it from the corner grocery store, and in consequence he needed a number of small buildings for storage and for the simple manufacturing processes of the farm which have now become obsolete. Nowadays practically the only dependencies on the small country place are the garage and such ornamental structures as may be needed to accentuate the features of the garden. Formerly the well equipped small farm had an extensive stable, cow barns, carriage house, sheds for tools and vehicles, a smoke-house, a summer kitchen, corn-cribs, summer-houses, chicken coops, well-heads, and another type of structure which I can best describe by telling how some elderly aunts of mine in remodeling an old farm-house (being delicately minded) talked to the contractor of the "cabinet"; when he made his drawings they were much surprised to find "cabin B" out in the back yard.

The quality and design of all these dependencies naturally varied very greatly with the means and tastes of the owners, but it is not infrequent to find small outbuildings in which the design is quite as careful as that of the house, and in complete conformity to its style. This was especially true of those outbuildings which were erected in the immediate vicinity of the house and were intimately related to the activities of the house. Stables for the owner's driving horses, for example, were usually placed near the house, often connected to it, especially in the northern part of New England, and were treated in much the same style as that of the house, although with a less degree of ornament.

A curious feature of these dependencies in Colonial times was that their design showed a surprising lack of adaptation to their purposes and little expression of the uses of the buildings. Certain features, notably the well-heads and summer-houses in the garden, were of such shapes and of such requirements that it was impossible, or at least difficult, to reproduce miniature houses. A trellised arbor, for example, in a garden is necessarily open to the breezes on all sides, and must afford a support for vines in order that it may properly fulfil its function. Summer-houses, therefore, have compelled the designers to display originality and ingenuity beyond the point they reached in many of the other buildings Even in these garden-houses there is a tendency to reproduce buildings or portions of buildings in miniature. This is not surprising if one stops to consider the methods of design in Colonial times. The architect as we know him to-day was practically non-existent, and for the most part the delightful Colonial houses were not drawn at all, but were just built, with the ornamental features such as doorways, cornices, windows, porches, etc., copied out of one of the books then in use, such as "Palladio Londinienses," or, later, Asher Benjamin's "Country Carpenter's Assistant." The men who were doing these houses had learned their mass proportion by experiment, the size of their windows was determined by available glass sizes, and all ornament copied, so that they probably used drawing instruments with difficulty, or not at all; and nobody can design without a pencil. Therefore, when they were forced to build garden structures of small size and without precedent or available designs, they copied either a small portion of some design at hand or reduced the scale of the book design to the required size. A notable example is the gazebo of the Royall house at Medford, Massachusetts, which was nothing but the crowning member of a church spire or the

BARN OF THE CAPTAIN ABRAHAM BURBANK HOUSE, SUFFIELD, CONNECTICUT.   Built about 1790.

DEPENDENCIES OF THE ANDREW B. HARRING HOUSE
AT NORTHVALE, NEW JERSEY.

DEPENDENCIES OF THE ROCKWELL HOUSE, WINSTED, CONNECTICUT.   Built in 1813.

Stable and West Approach.

THE DE WOLF-MIDDLETON HOUSE, PAPASQUE NECK, BRISTOL, RHODE ISLAND.

cupola of a public building set upon a raised mound. It is extremely entertaining, but one unquestionably has the feeling that the building upon which it rests has disappeared into the earth through some cataclysm of nature, and one would expect to be able to excavate a buried Pompeii or a New England city of Ys from the ground below. One of these garden structures which is doubtless perfectly familiar to every architect is the tea-house of the Derby estate. Naturally a little building so amusing and so characteristically Colonial as this would not escape frequent publication, but since its design illustrates so well the point I want to make, I cannot refrain from mentioning it in this sketch. The first floor of the building was intended for the storage of tools, and the second floor for a summer-house or tea-house, but the design is really that of a public building for a colony of dolls rather than of a garden structure pure and simple.

Toward the end of the Colonial period our ancestors began using little models of Greek temples for houses, and obsessed with the idea that one must have a Greek temple or nothing, they built even their dependencies in this characteristic fashion. The spring-house of the Goodloe Harper

Gazebo of the
ROYALL HOUSE, MEDFORD, MASSACHUSETTS.

THE ELIAS H. DERBY TEA-HOUSE AT
PEABODY, MASSACHUSETTS.

house, near Baltimore, Maryland, is a most excellent example; and on the North Country Road near Massapequa, Long Island, there is a very pleasant Greek temple house with a sort of baby temple alongside, the baby temple having been used as an office for the owner of the estate. It is curious among early architects, as illustrated in this Massapequa house, to find that a considerable alteration of scale apparently troubled the designer not at all. What he was after was a similar design regardless of the scale, and very frequently we find cases of similar treatment of different sizes of buildings. The barn of "Vesper Cliff," at Owego, New York, might be taken for a small church if one didn't know that it was used for a barn, but on the other hand the barn of the Burbank house, at Suffield, Connecticut, has been designed with large entrances, is in scale with the house, and is a mighty attractive building as well. Designs such as this were the exception rather than the rule with the early architects; at least I have seen comparatively few examples either in reality or in photographs; which probably accounts for the familiarity of the few remaining examples, such as the stable of the Pierce - Nichols house, at Salem, a

BARN AT "VESPER CLIFF," OWEGO, NEW YORK,
JOHNSON-PLATT HOUSE. Built about 1830.

very pleasant piece of architecture, and very distinctly a stable, although quite at one in character with the house to which it is attached. A similar instance will occur to the members of the American Institute of Architects in the stable of the Octagon, at Washington.

The stable of the Pierce-Nichols house is the only country example which occurs to me of the common European stable form, in which the stable was built around a central court, and there existed even in the cities comparatively few examples of this pleasant form of construction.

THE ROCKWELL HOUSE, WINSTED, CONNECTICUT.

Its origin was doubtless due to the medieval necessity for protection against enemies, but our climate is quite as great an enemy as a band of robbers, and one which is always with us, so it is surprising to find so few instances of large stable groups planned in this logical and traditional fashion. Its obvious advantages of the protection against wind and snow would seem sufficient so that our Colonial ancestors, with their many horses and cattle, would have selected it for much country work, instead of planning their farm buildings in a row, as was usually the

Dependencies of the
BACON HOUSE, KENT, CONNECTICUT.

perhaps of all these examples is that at Winsted, Connecticut, where a little group, consisting of the carriage house and "cabin B," was built at the rear of the farm-house, the farm-house cornice being followed at the same scale on the carriage house, and same design duplicated at a reduced scale carried on pigmy pilasters on the "cabin."

There was a certain class of dependencies which has not been previously mentioned but which had a real bearing on modern architecture, and that is the slave quarters, common throughout the South and even fairly frequent in the Middle States and New England. I imagine that most Northern people and many Southern people do not realize that the last slaves held in the United States were in the State of Delaware in 1867, and that slavery in Connecticut was not abolished until some years after the Revolution. These slave quarters were, especially in the Northern States, often of substantial and attractive construction, suitable for precedent for the small country cottages of to-day, and a sort of natural ancestor of

case. Nor was its size alone sufficient to cause its relinquishment; most farms needed sufficient buildings to enclose a court, and my only explanation is that the Colonial farm groups were in most cases aggregations of buildings erected when necessity impelled, rather than designed or even mentally provided for in advance by the owners.

In buildings of the farm-house type it was very common to place certain dependencies in a wing of the building or in a separate structure attached to the main building by a covered passageway. Many of the quaintest and most attractive old Dutch farm-houses were treated in this manner, the Andrew B. Harring house, at Northvale, New Jersey, being a typical Middle States example, partially of stone and partially of wood; while the Bacon house, at Kent, Connecticut, is typical of New England. It may be said in general that the farther north one goes the more frequently these dependencies were connected to the house by an interior passage, and what was occasional in Connecticut became customary in New Hampshire and Vermont. One of the most amusing

Courtyard.
THE PIERCE-NICHOLS HOUSE, SALEM, MASSACHUSETTS.

the superintendent's or gardener's cottage of large estates. The example illustrated at Woodbury, Connecticut, is now used as a tea-house, and is interesting as showing not only the house itself but also an amusing example of a well covering, although the well covering has no claims to architectural merit. I am sorry to see the old wellhead disappear, although I am glad that our drinking water no longer comes from the wells; but such a one as that of East Greenwich, Rhode Island, illustrated on page fourteen, is an extremely picturesque feature of the

Stable and Woodshed.
HOUSE AT PORTSMOUTH, NEW HAMPSHIRE.

country place, and one which we are, alas, no longer called upon to design. The Colonial designer of this well-head was able to free himself from the desire to duplicate in miniature the motives of the house. The building is of course not much bigger in size than the largest piece of Colonial furniture, and in design the designer has considered furniture precedent rather than outdoor construction. The cornice resembles the cornice of the old kitchen cabinets or of corner cupboards rather than that of a house, and is,

of course, much better adapted in scale and in profile to act as a crowning mass than would be the typical classic cornice. The well-head in this country never reached the interest and beauty of many of the European examples, in which masonry and wrought-iron work were so freely employed, but our old well-heads did have a quality of their own, and the fact that they were constructed of wood painted white, very often with green louvers, gave one a feeling that the water within was pure, cool, and sparkling, such as no nickel-plated faucet or white lavatory can inspire. It is too bad that the old quaint customs were so often inconvenient or unsanitary, and that as most wellheads covered dug wells of little depth the water was often apt to be polluted from the drainage of the house.

Of the many charming examples of garden architecture left to us from Colonial times it seems unnecessary to speak at length. There was a surprising similarity in their design from Maine to South Carolina. The use of trellised arches for roses and other climbing vines was a common feature to mark

Old Slave Quarters of the
BACON HOUSE, WOODBURY, CONNECTICUT.

WELL-HEAD AT
EAST GREENWICH,
RHODE ISLAND

the entrance to the garden. The turns of the paths were very frequently covered by summerhouses of square or octagonal shape, with ingenious variations in the trellis and treatment of the hoods. These were sometimes open and trellised, sometimes closed and shingled, and in some cases portions of the roof were left open while the center part was covered. They became almost automatically a feature of every Colonial garden; sometimes only a place on which flowers or grapes could be grown and sometimes a genuine gazebo, but always

Outhouse.
FORT JOHNSON HOUSE, AMSTERDAM, NEW YORK.

the interest of the gardens of which they formed a part was greatly enhanced by their white-painted or whitewashed outlines gleaming through the shrubbery and flowers. They are the best evidences, I think, that our ancestors were able to design in a more or less playful spirit and that the dour New England conscience was unable to resist the pleasure and brightness of its gardens. New Englanders were flower lovers, if we ever had flower lovers, and it is a pleasant thing to remember, especially in these days when the New England con-

SUMMER-HOUSE AT NEWBURYPORT, MASSACHUSETTS.

purity and refinement of composition together with great ingenuity in making slight fundamental variations of design.

When one considers the variety of uses to which the dependencies of Colonial buildings were put, one is surprised to find their design so generally similar to that of the dwelling-house. It would seem that the very factors which made for the extraordinarily high quality of taste in ornament and of correctness in mass in Colonial work tended to confine the imagination of the Colonial designers. It is well to remember that architectural design is necessarily limited within rather narrow bounds by the limitations of tradition and precedent; that in Colonial days there were few precedents; and that the knowledge of precedent, other than Classic, was practically none. So, in judging the work of the early American designers we must realize that their minds ran in narrow but exceedingly deep grooves of tradition, and we should not be surprised that their work was so uniform, either in the type of design or in its quality. We are accustomed to attribute to these early American designers a greater average ability than they possessed, because their work was so consistently excellent.

science has become a thing to be ashamed of rather than admired.

One dependency of the Colonial house I do not find among this collection of illustrations, the grape arbor. Our Colonial ancestors not only liked flowers, but also, I am pleased rather than regretful to say, liked the pressed juice of the grape after it had been kept for a while and put in casks or bottles; so to the Italian pergola precedent we have added the American grape arbor as a boundary motive to our estates or gardens.

As in Colonial work in general, we find a rather narrow range of architecture in the dependencies of the Colonial houses. I always think of Greek and Colonial architecture as having in common that both styles were perfected within narrow limits, set possibly by their ignorance of many precedents, possibly by the purity of their tastes. As the Colonial builders and the Greeks alike were compelled to use ornament sparingly, its use became quite an event, and its design and execution were thoroughly studied. Again the architecture of both periods depends upon the masses of the structures and the refinement and position of their moldings rather than upon elaborate composition or complicated detail; so we find in Colonial as in Greek a

Old Terraced Garden, back of the Barn.
THE PIERCE-NICHOLS HOUSE, SALEM, MASSACHUSETTS.

SUMMER-HOUSE IN THE ENDICOTT GARDEN,
DANVERS, MASSACHUSETTS.

223